Navigation for the Soul

Navigation for the Soul

Your Guide on the Path
From Darkness to Light

Geri Burke, MSEE, MSIE, Reiki Master

GTVentures
- Publishing -

Published by G.T. Ventures, LLC
2000 Cheney Highway
Suite 103-290
Titusville, FL 32780

ISBN: 978-1-7361172-0-0

To everyone who is struggling,
may this book help you finally steer toward your light.

Hell is to drift; heaven is to steer.
—George Bernard Shaw
Man and Superman

Illustrations

Figures

Tables

Contents

Acknowledgments

There have been so many people without whom I might never have healed enough to write this book.

To Gary—my husband, my lover, my friend: From the moment we met, and even when we were miles apart, you were right by my side. As I struggled to heal, as I searched for myself and how to communicate who I had become to the world, you believed in me. Thank you. Forever and a day, I love you.

To my brother, Steve Burke: Throughout this journey, you have been there when I needed someone who understood the truth. You didn't try to give me solutions; instead, you seemed to know that letting me just cry was all I really needed. You called it the *rinse cycle,* and I loved that you would patiently wait until all the tears stopped before making me laugh. I think you and I hold the record for the longest brother-and-sister phone call.

To Gwen Shangle: You were the light of my childhood and the piece of my heart that I turned to when I needed to breathe. You believed in me when I couldn't believe in myself. Thank you for bringing matching pajamas and just sitting with me when I was so sick. And thank you for being my little sister.

To Penny Austin: You have been so much in my life, more than a friend, more than a sister; you let me cry when I was so full of pain, and you comforted me like the mother I never had. I already miss you so much it hurts. I hope you know how much I will always love you.

To Patricia Trosino: Your friendship and faith in my work kept me moving forward on this journey. You are so much more than my husband's mom; you are a fellow pilgrim, living your life with purpose and according to the holy guiding light.

To Shannon Gronich: Thank you for asking about the diagram I had on the little whiteboard on my fridge. The contents of this book began on that little whiteboard, and you were the first one to hear me explain how it worked. Thank you for loving it and making it real for the first time.

To Nancy Matthews: I knew from the moment we met that we were on the same mission. It was that light in your eyes, a knowing that you knew the secret too. Your friendship gave me gentle strength to finally speak my truth.

To my mom: I know you were raised in a different time and that you did the best you could with the reality you knew. Writing this book helped me to heal both my "self" and my relationship with you. I love you. Without you as my mom, this book might not have been written.

And to Keith and Maura Leon at Babypie Publishing for being so patient with me as I released this book—one white knuckle at a time— thank you. I knew from the moment we met that there was something important we were meant to do together. Who knew it would take so long! I love you both and am blessed to call you my friends.

Foreword

Geri and I first met at a Women's Prosperity Network (WPN) event. As cofounder of WPN, it is my purpose and my pleasure to serve women right where they are, by being *the one* for them and knowing that our paths have crossed because they are *the one* for me as well. Geri was walking with a cane, and I could see that she was having difficulty keeping her balance as well as having some difficulty communicating. She spoke timidly and quietly to the others at the event. And although she sat in the back of the room and kept to herself, it was clear to me that she wanted to be there with us. I could see a light in her eyes that drew me to her in some way.

At one point, she asked me for a few minutes of my time—asked if I would come over to her table so that she could speak with me. I said that I would, and when everyone else had gone to lunch, I went to the back of the room where she was sitting, and she told me her story. It was an amazing story—what she had been through, what she had survived, and what she knew she was meant to do.

She told me that she had had a third-degree heart block and sudden cardiac arrest only eighteen months earlier. When her heart had stopped and she crossed over, she experienced the face of God and was given the instruction to come back and share something with the world. She felt that our group was where she was meant to be, to help her fulfill that mission.

I was completely blown away. While I had been wondering what had happened to her, I was not expecting that she had come back from the dead.

[In] the two years that followed our first meeting, I saw Geri fight her way back, put that cane away, speak in front of people, share her story, and share her message.

And now she has asked me to write a foreword for her for her first book. Again, I am blown away.

This book is the message that Geri was sent back to give to humanity. It is instruction for us to be spiritual beings in a physical world. This book outlines the system that we were all given, the system for us to use to be guided by spirit, to live a joyful life and to connect with others in order to fulfill God's purpose of creating heaven on Earth.

I was fascinated that this book is more than just an inspirational story of how Geri survived many traumas and became the inspiration she is today. This book gives the instruction on how to navigate your life using the body, mind, and soul that you were given as the controls for moving through your life and according to your higher purpose.

And, it is so much more. Geri weaves her story through the pages and through the chapters, giving real-life experiences and showing the depth of her understanding of the pain that humanity is going through. Written any other way, it might have been almost too painful to read, but instead she presents these experiences with such light and love that it is clear that she has been touched by the light of God. And through these chapters, Geri defines and describes the process we must go through to take steps forward in alignment and according to our higher purpose.

Since Geri had been an engineer for nearly thirty years, the book is well organized. But it is also simple and easy to read with clear descriptions and examples. It is broken into nine sections, each beginning with a personal story from Geri's life. The first section is a description of the tool, which has seven parts. The next seven sections of the book take the reader through each of those parts, again, beginning with a supporting story from her life, then describing where each component exists in your physical body and is used by the navigation system. Then, Geri teaches a simple way to work with and improve the health of that piece. The way Geri describes how she uses each of these seven components within her own life is refreshingly open and honest. She describes where it can be used in your personal life, in your career, or in your business.

My favorite part of the book is where Geri describes specific actions you can take to focus on each piece and improve its function so that it helps the entire navigation process work better. Each function has a simple mantra that can be spoken; a color to focus on; herbs and oils to stimulate the sense of smell; a tone that can be used to stimulate your sense of hearing and the vibrations around you; sounds found in nature, like running water, musical instruments, the sound of violins; certain crystals that align with that part of the navigation tool; an easy exercise; and finally, a simple meditation on which you can focus your prayers and the archangel whose job it is to help with the function of that area. These suggestions give you, the reader, something specific you can do, actions you can take. By doing so, you gain a sense of control and momentum toward a better life.

This book has a feminine energy to it as Geri talks about allowing, flow, and ease. She speaks of the dance between your divinely guided life and the divine energy of our cosmic consciousness. It is a gentle book and a book that you will cherish for years to come. One suggestion is to play the tone associated with the section you are reading while you are reading that section.

At the end of each chapter, Geri lists a key point to focus on and a specific action step to take in order to reinforce the ideas covered in the chapter. She also suggests that the first time you read the book, read only one chapter per day at most, and spend time focusing on the key point and action steps for only that chapter. I couldn't agree more. It is a powerful practice.

While reading this book, I began thinking about how powerful our thoughts are and how difficult it can be to control our thoughts. This book showed me how to focus my thoughts on specific areas of my body in a very actionable way, to use those areas of my body like I use a steering wheel in a car. It showed me where in my body I actually receive guidance from Source and where I can take that guidance and turn it into action, all by focusing on the places in my body that make up the navigation tool.

Anyone who wants to take control of their life will benefit greatly by reading this book, especially if they are struggling with understanding how what they have been through is affecting them today as an adult. Read this book. Study this book. Take it with you. Use the guidance within this book to receive your own guidance and navigate your life according to your highest purpose. This is the gift that Geri has brought back.

Nancy Carr Matthews
International Speaker, Best-Selling Author, Global Leader
Founder, Women's Prosperity Network

Introduction

It has taken me a long time to finally sit down and put this book together. I use the words *putting it together* because it has been inside of me for years, perhaps my whole life. It was a hunger wanting to be fed the only way it could be fed, by putting everything else in my life to the side, picking up a pen, and beginning.

My life hasn't been easy, but I bet you've heard that before. Maybe my life has been harder than most, maybe not as hard as others. One thing I know: There were times that I thought I wouldn't make it to another day.

When I was three years old, my father built a bomb shelter in our backyard. I remember the rumbling of the big machine as it dug a huge hole in the ground, pulling up grass and deep brown dirt and rocks. Even at that early age, I could sense that life would never be the same for my family; something didn't feel safe. It was more than not safe because of the heavy-handed discipline that was commonplace behind our closed doors. This was something outside our house, and I could sense that it even scared the grown-ups.

The man who dug that giant hole didn't talk much as he pulled on the levers of the mechanical beast. Each savage thrust of the machine he controlled was intentional, squealing and screeching and vibrating as if he were ripping apart an injured animal.

The next memory was of my father building a jungle gym on top of where that hole in the earth used to be. I don't remember the concrete being poured to seal the bunker. I don't remember anyone talking about how, when the day comes, we should run for our lives, down a ladder and into a hole in the ground. Instead, on top of where that hole had been, there was a small playground, and my father was helping me swing from the homemade monkey bars. I remember his tank T-shirt, his cropped hair, his smile. There was nothing to be afraid of, not with my dad to protect me and all my brothers and sisters to play with.

I never told anyone about the nightmares. The theme was always about the end of the world, a nuclear holocaust, and everyone I loved had melted and morphed into something unrecognizable because of the radiation. They would look at me in my dream, begging me with their eyes to stop the pain and searching for answers: *Why?*

I would wake up, drenched with sweat and heart racing, confused that the world suddenly seemed normal. Everyone was going about their business as if nothing were wrong, and there was nothing to fear. But deep inside, I was terrified. There was something ominous in the air, something thick. I felt just one step ahead of a monster that could pull me down into the hell that turned people into disfigured, pain-ridden creatures.

Then the Vietnam war was broadcast live on our television while we ate dinner. The announcers talked about body counts; magazines showed a naked girl running down the street in tears, her clothes burned off her small body. They showed a man being shot in the head while begging for his life. College students were rioting, and young men were burning their draft cards.

At the same time, there were race riots, assassinations, and shortages of sugar, coffee, and chocolate. During the oil crisis, we were allowed to put gas in our car only every other day. Everything seemed surreal, as if at any moment my loved ones would begin to melt. There was danger everywhere, but we were expected to smile and go about our day as if everything were normal.

I was raised with trauma. I lived the first half of my life with trauma. Physical, emotional, and sexual abuse against women was the norm and permeated my life until I finally told someone who could help me. I was thirty years old when I realized that my life could be different. I hadn't realized the damage I had sustained. Even though I worked through the emotional aspects of my past, my body was still overreacting to stress, except now the stress was environmental.

In 2004, the year after we moved to Florida, we were hit with four hurricanes in a row. Our home received only minor damage, but the old buildings that I worked in were a different story. When we finally returned to work, there was still standing water in the hallways, and you could hear water flowing behind some of the walls. The carpets squished under our feet for weeks, but nobody ever came to replace them or the drywall.

Mold grew everywhere. Bats took up residence in the air handler above my office. The buildings were dirty and had no windows to let in the fresh air.

Over the years that followed, the sick buildings became a sick joke around the campus. I had no idea how sick they were because I didn't know that the entire 140-acre campus had been declared a super-fund site in 1987. When the hurricanes hit, the company was in the middle of cleaning up the site, but it took another five years to be within safe levels.

It is no wonder that so many people feel trapped. Our bodies are designed to hide from danger. The probability of surviving increases if you stay with what is familiar. Thousands of years ago, we were hiding in the bushes and in the caves.

Today, there are modern-day dangers of losing our job and being out on the street. We hide in our cubicles and consume fear through the media. It is no wonder that Wall Street feeds on the fear of the crowds. This is how we were raised. The fear is somehow familiar to us, makes us feel secure. This is how I was raised, with a twisted sense of safety.

When I started feeling really sick with heart flutters and skips, it didn't occur to me that my childhood trauma could be the cause. Doctor after doctor couldn't find anything wrong, couldn't find a reason why I was having trouble breathing, no answers to the rashes, the hoarse voice, the choking sensations, the feeling that my heart was skipping beats. I tried to tell them that I thought all these symptoms were related, but they just kept telling me that they couldn't find anything wrong.

So, I pushed forward. And I pushed more. The more I pushed, the sicker I felt. The sicker I felt, the more I felt the need to push forward because there were bills to pay and pushing forward was what I did best.

Then, I began getting this nagging feeling, like something wasn't quite right. I couldn't put my finger on what was bothering me. It got stronger and clearer. I told my husband that something didn't feel right, that I felt like my life had to change. I felt I was doing it all wrong: my career, all the bills, all of the stress. I felt I was being strongly guided by God, that I was receiving something from above.

There it was again, louder, stronger: *Don't shrink back! They need you!*

It was the little girl I used to be, knowing I was shrinking back and wanting me to be strong, in spite of her still being so afraid. She wanted me to begin the journey. I knew that she would follow, always a few steps behind, in the shadows.

My rational brain took over and told me that there were bills to pay, and I couldn't see a way to just drop everything to follow a whisper.

One day, my heart just stopped beating. It was a third-degree heart block, a sudden cardiac arrest. I flatlined and went to a place where I remembered truth. We all know the truth; we just forget that we know. Instead, we think that the truth is too simple. We think that others will laugh at us and think we are crazy if we just live our truth.

Instead, we capitulate and swirl about, hindered by how we have been hurt and wronged, and we waste our lives. We think we are alone—that there is nothing that we can reach out to for help. We swim against the current of our lives, trying to climb up and out of what we think is a raging river, not realizing that we are meant to just lie back and float.

The whispers I had been hearing were real, and I had work to do. I had to come back, and I knew what I needed to do.

There is a direct connection between our physical (biologic), our emotional (thought), and our energetic (spiritual) bodies. The physiological term related to this connection is the *hypothalamic-pituitary-adrenal axis* (HPA-Axis). This body/mind/soul relationship is altered when we experience trauma as an adult and stunted if we experience chronic trauma early in life, when the HPA-axis is developing.[1]

The consequence is *hypothalamic-pituitary-adrenal axis dysregulation* (HPA-D) and autonomic nervous system hyperreactivity. The person becomes hypervigilant and hypersensitive to all forms of stress. They become fear averse, stuck in what some call the *upper limit*. Climbing out of that existence is like trying to drive a car through dense fog on a strange road without GPS to help you navigate. A common coaching strategy says "Feel the fear and do it anyway," but this is completely unrealistic and perhaps not even possible for those with HPA-D.

Some of us use GPS to travel across town, along roads that we have traveled a hundred times before. Some of us use GPS to explore places we have never been. I was a GPS navigation engineer for twenty-eight years, and I knew that with the knowledge I had gained from my near-

---

1 Klaassans, Ellen R. "Bouncing Back: Trauma and the HPA-Axis in Healthy Adults." *Eur J Psychotraumatol.* 2010, 1:1. dx.doi.org/10.3402%2Fejpt.v1i0.5844 dx.doi.org/10.3402%2Fejpt.v1i0.5844

death experience (NDE), I could create a tool to help people navigate their lives.

This book is about that tool. It helps you move forward if you feel stuck, lost, or overwhelmed. It is a GPS for your very soul.

As I have developed this tool, I've used it to get me through my healing and recovery. I've used it to get me through ordinary days too. It has both kept me calm and brought me back to calm. It has given me clarity. It has made me strong. It has made the little girl I used to be smile. But most of all, it has given me back my life. I no longer act just to survive; I live the life I was meant to live.

The tool is based on a radio frequency (RF) receiver, which is used by mobile phones, radios, and GPS navigation systems to take signals out of the airways and turn them into something that we can understand.

From my NDE, I realized we are meant to receive heavenly guidance. The angels send us guidance to help us live the lives we are meant to live.

We are meant to live lives of joy.

We are meant to ask for guidance to get through difficult times

We are meant to ask for guidance to fill our souls with passion and purpose.

If you ask yourself right now whether this is true, you will know that it is.

This book is broken up into sections and short chapters. At the end of each chapter, you will see the symbols shown below. Take a moment at the end of each chapter to reflect on the **Action Steps**. Instead of going immediately to the next chapter, perhaps take a full day to understand how you feel about what you have read before moving on.

🌱 **KEY POINT** The main concept to remember from this section.

👣 **ACTION STEPS** Activities you can do in the moment to help reinforce the key point. Get a journal to record your thoughts and experiences as you go and have it handy while you read and try the action steps.

For He will give His angels charge of you to guard you in all your ways.
　　　　　　　　　　　—Psalm 91:11 (RSAVCE)

The Tool

The Tool and the Truth

A radio frequency (RF) receiver takes wireless signals out of the airways and turns those signals into information we can understand. A mobile phone turns wireless signals into audible voice signals and sends them to the speaker so you can hear what the person said. It is so seamless that you don't even realize that the voice you are hearing is a reconstruction of what they said a fraction of a second earlier. A radio turns a wireless signal into music. The RF receiver in a GPS navigation system turns a wireless signal into a direction command.

There are seven components to an RF receiver:

1. Antenna – receives the wireless signal.

2. High-Pass Filter – only allows high frequency energy to pass through and sends low frequency energy to ground.

3. Ground – sends unwanted energies out of the system and into the Earth.

4. Oscillator – vibrates at a lower harmonic of the desired wireless signal.

5. Mixer – combines the received wireless signal with the lower harmonic resonance of the oscillator. The result is that the wireless signal is copied from the very high frequency to the lower harmonic frequencies. This mixing process creates multiple copies.

6. Band-Pass filter – a filter is needed for all but one copy of the received signal. All other copies and any interference signals are sent to ground.

7. Output – the resulting signal is a replica of the wireless signal but at a lower frequency than can be heard or seen.

You have all these components within you:

1. Antenna – your pineal gland acts as an antenna. There is an energy center *(chakra),* called the *crown chakra,* that is associated with your pineal gland.

2. High-Pass Filter – your pituitary gland acts as a high-pass filter. The energy center associated with the pituitary gland is called the *third eye chakra.* You can use the wisdom of your third eye chakra to let only high-frequency guidance enter your thoughts.

3. Ground – your adrenal glands are made up of the *adrenal cortex,* or the outside layer, and the *adrenal medulla,* or the core. The adrenal medulla acts as a ground. There is an energy center associated with it called the *root chakra.*

4. Oscillator – your thymus gland acts as an oscillator. The energy center associated with your thymus gland is called the *heart chakra.*

5. Mixer – your thyroid gland acts as a mixer. The energy center associated with your thyroid gland is called the *throat chakra.*

6. Band-Pass filter – your reproductive glands act as a band-pass filter. The energy center associated with these glands, called the *sacral chakra,* acts as a band-pass filter.

7. Output – your pancreas acts as an RF output. There is an energy center associated with the pancreas called the *solar plexus chakra,* which acts as an RF output.

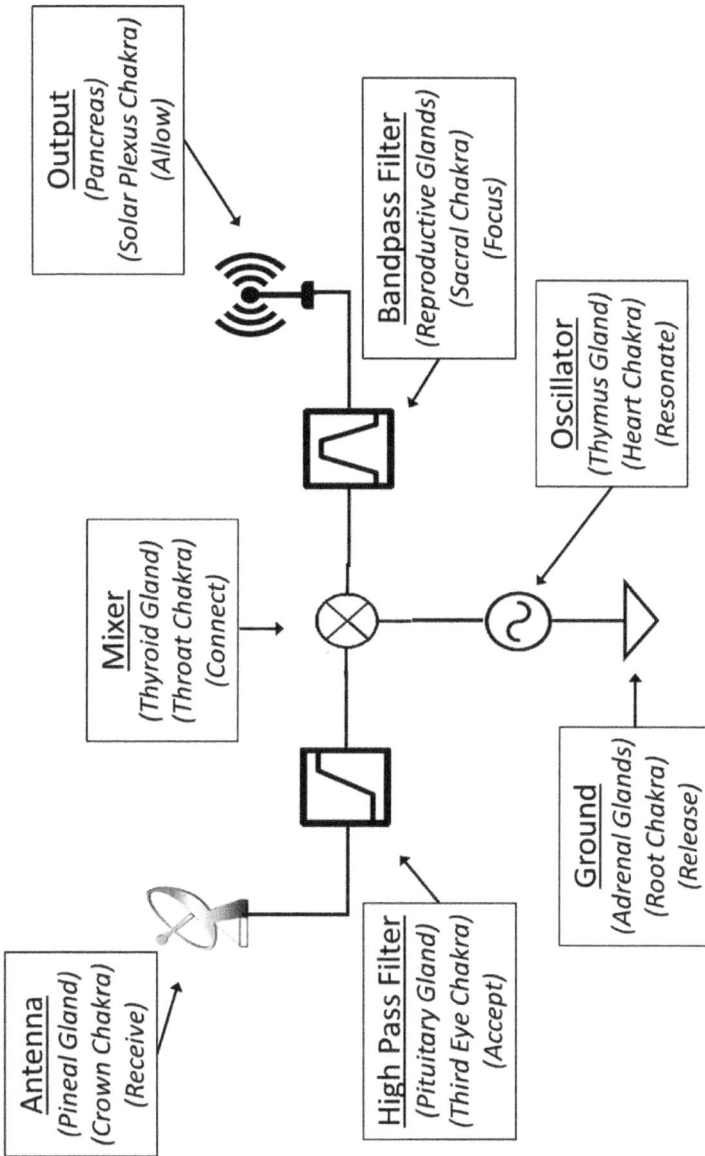

Figure 1 Navigation for the Soul Uses a GPS Receiver

You can apply these areas to navigating your life, empowering yourself to live a life that will make your soul happy: starting a business, enhancing a career, creating a movement, or making huge change in the world.

1. Antenna – receive spiritual guidance from Source and the angels (vision and purpose).

2. High-Pass Filter – accept the truth of the guidance (mission).

3. Ground – release what has been holding you back (be yourself, be).

4. Oscillator – resonate gratitude and love (resonate with the truth of your soul's message).

5. Mixer – connect with humanity and speak your truth (share your message).

6. Band-Pass filter – focus on the next step you are being guided to take (make a plan).

7. Output – take courageous action (follow your plan).

It is time for you to make a difference. It is time for you to accept your power and use that power to lift the eyes of those who are searching for help to raise their vibration and their hope. It starts with you. It is time.

🌱 KEY POINT

Each one of us has all the components we need to act as an RF receiver to receive guidance and to process that guidance in a way that we can take action according to Source.

👣 ACTION STEP

Place your right hand on top of your head and your left hand over your heart. Close your eyes and visualize a white light entering the top of your head through your right hand. Feel your heart glowing warmly through your left hand with the warmth of love energy. With the strength of your mind, accept that you are being guided by all that is holy and feel the guidance connect to your physical world. Release any thoughts of doubt and focus on the truth that the steps you will take will be in accordance with that guidance. Open your eyes and go about your day, knowing that you have been guided, and all is well.

Write or draw in your journal what you want to remember of this experience.

Receive

My Personal Navigation

The first time I felt my heart flutter and skip, it startled me. It felt like dread. From somewhere both deep inside me, yet still far away, I felt more than heard a warning. I was standing just outside our patio door, waiting for our rottweiler, Tasmine, to relieve herself. It was a normal night, although a bit cool for April in Florida. The smell of orange blossoms was in the air. They were my favorite, much better than honeysuckles, which had been my favorite and something I missed terribly since leaving Pennsylvania eight years earlier.

The sensation was as if my heart had dropped an inch in my chest. It had become very still for a moment before resuming its normal beating as if nothing had happened. And yet, something had.

It is like the feeling you get when you know someone is standing behind you, even though you can't see them and haven't heard them. You know they are there. I knew something had happened with my heart. So did Tasmine, because she was suddenly there, next to me, looking up with a worried face as I leaned against the frame of the door. But in my usual fashion, I brushed it off and forgot about it. There were things to do. I was busy!

I did mention it to my doctor. She would listen to my heart and say it was beating with a normal rhythm. She would tell me to inhale as she listened to my lungs and then tell me I wasn't wheezing, but she never listened to me exhale. She never listened to me explain what was happening. The doctors all brushed me off; I felt completely ignored. And when I tried to push the issue, I was treated like a hypochondriac.

Finally, I went to Mayo in Jacksonville, where a cardiologist prescribed a two-week heart monitor, and a pulmonologist did a lung function test. Those results and those doctors told me how sick I really was. Two days after my idiopathic illness was confirmed, I collapsed, coughing up softball-sized blood clots. My oxygen had dropped below 78 percent and I had a 105-degree fever. The diagnosis was pneumonitis. The cause was a hypersensitive airway.

They never figured out what I was hypersensitive to, but after steroids, good antibiotics, and ten days in the hospital, my lungs were clear. I was told to go back to work. Even though I still felt so sick, the company doctor said that the tests showed I wasn't sick any longer, and hypersensitivity was just asthma.

Then HR said that I would be terminated if I didn't return to work.

That was the day that I broke down in tears, the moment I felt I had hit rock bottom. I was in my car, driving, stopped at a stoplight around the corner from my home. I gave in to my burden completely. With tears streaming down my face, I threw my arms up and prayed, "Dear God, I can't do this anymore, please help me!" I was at the bottom of everything—no strength left, no answers, no strategies, no options. I felt abandoned by God. I was exhausted. I begged God for a sign.

When I realized drivers in the cars behind me were leaning on their horns, and that I had been sitting there crying long after the light had turned green, I opened my eyes, looked to my right, and saw a big blue sign that said: Gabriel. It was at that moment that I knew God was with me. That sign had not been there the previous day. It was a campaign sign. The last name of the man running for office was Gabriel. But I knew that God had planned this encounter to show me that He was there for me. He was always there.

When I got home, I was still so full of the Holy Spirit that I took immediate action on the first guidance that came to me. I picked up my cell phone, opened Google, and searched for "Archangel Gabriel healing." It wasn't long before I found that 528 Hz is known as the miracle tone for healing. The frequency has a deep mathematical connection to the patterns of nature and is known as the frequency of love. Then I found an hour-long recording of the 528 Hz tone. I lay on the couch, placed the cell phone on my chest, and played that recording.

As the 528 Hz frequency vibrated through my chest cavity, I could feel the inflammation in and around my heart and lungs begin to resonate. I knew that I was in the hands of God.

The vibration relaxed me so completely and so quickly that I don't remember much, but when I awoke, I felt well. It was absolutely amazing! The depth of exhaustion was gone. I could breathe without pain.

I walked into the bathroom feeling very different. I wasn't alone. I looked into the mirror and felt that there were two of us looking at me in the mirror. Within me, there was someone else. My immediate thought was that it was Gabriel. It was crazy, but it was beautiful! I felt him smile at me.

And just like that, I was able to go back to work.

I stayed away from the buildings that had been triggering me, as instructed by the cardiologist. In fact, I spent most of that year working from my laptop in the courtyard. One of the benefits of living in Florida and having Wi-Fi accessible from outside the buildings was that I could stay in the fresh air. When I did have to go inside those buildings, I wore a 1-micron mask as instructed by the pulmonologist.

That is how I kept my job. For over a year until the new, clean building was ready, I worked from outside. Yes, my company was building a new building. I wasn't the only one having trouble breathing.

While I sat in the courtyard, I was able to talk to everyone who passed by me. I was no longer tucked away in an office down a long corridor. Instead, I was smiling and waving at people. I was seeing them and talking to them. And they were talking to me. They were sharing their struggles with me, how they felt so stuck in their lives. One man was writing a fiction novel at night after his wife and children were asleep. Another wanted to live in Italy and play his guitar, but his wife thought he was crazy. Another wanted to design garden kits and send them to people who were hungry so they could grow a few vegetables and feed themselves. Another simply wanted to serve as a finance coach to help those who were struggling with debt. Another had invented a method to skim plastic sludge off the surface of the water and just needed investors so he could quit this job and fulfill his purpose in this lifetime.

They all wanted more meaning in the time they had left. They all felt the work they were doing in their jobs was not the work they were meant to do, but it paid the bills, so they were trapped.

It was just amazing the things we talked about. I felt so full of love; the clarity was just incredible. I was there for them, in the moment. I was, but it was Gabriel who guided me. It felt so beautiful.

I was one of the very first to move into the new building. It was beautiful, with co-creating spaces designed so interaction between the engineers would inspire innovation. The conversations were so stimulating

And, I could take off the mask!

So, I wasn't wearing the mask when the water treatment plant next door shut down and cleaned their vats. I wasn't wearing the mask when the main air handler pulled in the fumes from the cleaning process. We all felt our eyes, nose, and throat burn, and I knew I had to get out of there. I was being told to quickly get out of there by whatever was within me. I thought I got out in time, but I didn't.

The signals that tell my heart to beat became erratic, and then stopped. It was a third-degree heart block and a sudden cardiac arrest.

I don't ignore that inner voice any longer. Ever. I don't brush it off as "nonsense" or just silly fear of moving forward. This inner voice of guidance may have been what saved my life more than once. But more than that, this guidance is what has saved my entire life by guiding my moments. Since my NDE, it has nudged me along the way, steering me toward living a life with more meaning. It has gently turned my head toward opportunities that give me more money, so that I can have more time to live my life with more meaning.

The rest is up to me. Faith.

Juggling Chainsaws

When I was a little girl, standing out was dangerous, and thriving meant hiding. I was born eighth in a family of ten children. It was loud: people yelled, threw objects in anger, and threw hurtful words in frustration. And worse, much worse.

When I was eleven, I finally got up the courage to tell my mother that my older brother was molesting me sexually. The sting of her slapping me across the face in response is something I will never forget. But it was her words that cut the deepest. She called me a liar. She told me that even if it did happen, I probably wanted it, and therefore, I was a whore and a slut. And then she took me to the doctor where he examined me while she watched. When he shook his head no, she threw my clothes at me and yelled at me to get dressed.

All the way home, she screamed at me so violently that spit came out of her mouth, "I always knew you were nothing but a dirty little slut."

So, I disappeared into a deep place within myself. Nobody knew I had gone. I looked the same as I had always looked, but I was not there.

My mother shunned me after that and instructed my siblings to turn against me as well. They might as well have been stoning me—their words were so harsh. But as if way down a tunnel, I could only see their lips moving; I couldn't hear what they said. They tried to make me cry, but I couldn't feel the belt, couldn't feel them hitting me, couldn't hear them screaming hurtful and hateful words.

I spent time in foster care because someone at school saw the bruises one day.

Keep quiet. Don't tell. Don't go against the family. Just accept that this is the way it is. It's not that bad. Forget what happened.

For most of my life, I was afraid to connect with the present—afraid to trust, afraid to put my feet on the ground for fear I would be hurt again, afraid I would lose control and everything would fall apart. The panic whispers I heard in the back of my head were incessant. To keep ahead of the fear, I tried to control everything. I kept my feet up and out of the swamp of my mind by keeping busy. If I took everything on, I could control everything. And if I worked really hard—if I didn't let my emotions show, didn't ever let anyone in completely—then things wouldn't fall apart.

I thought I appeared successful. I worked at a great job and made great money. But the truth is that I was a workaholic, and like every addict, I used my drug of choice to block out the pain. And still, that panic spilled through. It seemed that all I was doing was worrying about how I was going to pay the mortgage, not only at the end of the month but in three months. I searched for worries to busy my mind and quiet the whispers of panic. I thought I was just (LOL—*just*) continuously adding to my plate to show the world how much I could juggle. It was a horrifying cycle.

I felt like I was juggling chainsaws. If I let even one of them fall, then my entire life would crash down around me.

A series of events brought everything to a stop. I had a third-degree heart block and a sudden cardiac arrest.

When my heart stopped beating, I crossed over. In an instant, I was floating in thick black velvet with a million bright stars singing songs of love to me. The melody of their angelic voices flowed through me and in me, and I was one of them. The love I had held hidden inside for so long was all that I was, and it poured out of my soul and joined theirs.

I finally understood; I finally remembered the truth. There is a deep knowledge inside all of us, a truth. We are born with that knowledge. It comes from God. But if we are hurt by those we depend on to protect and care for us, then we become overwhelmed by fear and doubt. We begin to doubt the truth, and we bury the knowledge. We hide from everything, including ourselves.

The truth is that, although life has difficult moments, our creator did not want the experience called *life* to be hard. God wants us to be happy. Life was intended to be a gift of expressions, a physical experience between spiritual beings. The other side is like the other side of the looking glass, with beautiful angels waiting for us to ask them for guidance. We are powerful beyond our dreams. By draining away negative feelings and following heavenly guidance, our lives will flow with ease and joy, even during times that might feel challenging and heartbreaking.

When I came back, I knew I had been given the opportunity to redefine my life, but I had no idea what my new life might look like and no idea how to begin making changes. But I knew that the first step was to ask for guidance.

🌱 KEY POINT

No matter how difficult life can be, the angels are always there to ask for guidance.

👣 ACTION STEPS

Think of one aspect of your life that feels too heavy for you to handle. Ask for guidance from the angels. Sit quietly with your eyes closed and say: *Please help me. This is too heavy for me to handle by myself, and I need your guidance.*

Something will pop into your mind. Do not push it away or think it is nonsense. Open your journal and write down what you have asked for help with. Note the guidance you may have received.

Asking for Guidance

Have you ever sat back and asked yourself why you are here, on this Earth and in this lifetime? Do you sometimes feel a yearning, a pulling, to do something different? Have you ever questioned who you are meant to become or what you are meant to be doing?

We all have the ability to see with our mind's eye. We all have a vision from within our soul that is connected to our Creator. It is this guidance from Source that provides the answers. All we have to do is ask and then have faith that the answers are there, waiting for us to receive them.

It's like when you are driving and scanning the car radio for something good to listen to. You have faith that you will find a decent station. You push the button and then wait to hear what comes through the speakers. If it isn't something you are interested in listening to, then you push the button again. But if it is a good song, you turn up the volume and usually smile. All the stations were out there in the airways, but only one of them was meant for you. It is up to you to scan through them until you find the one that makes you smile.

When you sit quietly, do you hear a million thoughts racing through your head? It is just like all the stations out there in the airways. It is up to you to scan through them until you find the one that makes you smile. There is one thought that will quiet all the other racing thoughts and make you smile. This is your vision and it will lead you to your purpose.

Your vision is a snapshot of your future; it is a lighthouse with a beacon for you to focus upon. It is time fast-forwarded to when you have already done the work, and you are living that purposeful life.

With a purpose that will give your life joy and a vision of what that life looks like, you now must act to make that life a reality. It is your mission to take these steps. You are being given guidance from Source to begin.

Success is a personal thing, different for each of us. What satisfies me deeply may not mean much to you, and what is important to you may hold little to no meaning for me. We are individuals; we are different for a reason. If we all felt the same way about everything, then there would be no reason to look for happiness. If we were all satisfied by the same things, then there would be no reason to search for happiness. All you would need to do is ask your neighbor what makes them happy, and you would know what would satisfy you.

Success is a journey; it is not a destination. It is a good thing that success is not a destination because, if there were a place or a point in time that was called *success*, then when you'd reach that point, there would be nothing left for you to work toward. The reason for living, the purpose for striving toward the next thing, is the search for happiness, the search for more.

Success is not about the material goods you own or the career you have achieved; it is about your happiness. Some people still think that success is about the position or the salary or the house or the car. While those acquisitions might feel good, the moment you realize they are yours, that feeling is short-lived. A truly successful life is about happiness, and happiness is not tangible. It cannot be labeled; it cannot be touched. It can only be described.

Your happiness is your choice. You get to describe what success means to you. Other people can bring you their happiness and share it with you, but they cannot create your happiness for you. That is your responsibility and it is your gift.

What gives your life meaning? When you have answered that question, you'll know what defines success for you. Your life consists of the meaning you give it, and that meaning depends on how you define *success* and *happiness*.

In the book *Start With Why*, Simon Sinek, a motivational speaker and author, explains that humans are motivated more by the purpose behind something than what they can gain from the thing itself. People are motivated by the reason behind the action much more than the result from taking the action. There is also a TED Talk by Sinek titled "It Starts With Why."

In the movie *City Slickers*, a few men go on a vacation to find meaning in their lives. An old cowboy gives them sage advice when he tells them that the meaning of life is "just one thing." But, he continues, that one thing is something you must figure out for yourself.

I believe the work we are here on this Earth to do begins with figuring out what that one thing is, the one thing that will give our life meaning and make our life feel successful to us.

More Time

Time is a limited resource. There are only twenty-four hours in a day. You cannot create more time. You can change the way you spend the time you have, which in turn changes how you sense the passing of time. When you decide how you want to spend your time and spend it doing only what you want, you will feel as though you have more time.

So, imagine if you were not at your job for ten hours a day. What could you be doing? What would you like to be doing? How do you want to spend your time?

More Meaning

Now that you have decided how you want to be spending your time in your newly designed life, what will give your life purpose? Even if you are living each normal day and each extraordinary day the way you described in the section above, doing so without meaning will cause it to seem dull.

What is the one thing that will make your life truly successful? Why will you do what you do in the time that you have now in this lifetime? If you redesign your life to spend your days doing only what you want to do, you can spend that time doing what gives your life more meaning.

More Money

If you had more money, then you could decide how to spend your day. You probably wouldn't spend your time in traffic, driving to a job you didn't like, where you would be miserable for eight or more hours only to spend another hour or so driving home. And when you finally got home, you wouldn't spend the little time you had left of your day worrying about bills or the economy. If you had more money, you would spend your day the way you described your perfect normal day.

Money gives you the ability to do this. Money gives your time more meaning.

Some of us have heard people say negative things about making money as if it is a bad thing. Perhaps you have heard that if you make a lot of money, you are a greedy person, or you've heard that money is evil. But you can accomplish more and help more people if you have more money. With the freedom to spend time the way you want, your accomplishments will give your life more meaning. It is nature's way for humans to want to give to others, but you cannot give what you do not have. Without that money, you may be suffering, which limits your ability to help others who may be suffering. We were not put on this beautiful Earth and into this gift of life to suffer.

Money is simply a tool that gives you more time so that you can live your life with more meaning. You still need to pay your bills, so you can't just stop making money. But you could make money *doing* that which gives your life meaning.

At first, this might seem impossible. But taking it step by step is the way to make it happen. As shown in the diagram below, begin by feeding the pig. Give the cute little guy more income and take less money from him by reducing your expenses. Start with your expenses and trim them down so that they fit within the percentages shown. Then look at ways you can make more income doing something you enjoy doing. It might mean asking for a raise, changing jobs, getting a second job, starting a small side business, joining an MLM (multi-level marketing) system, learning to invest for income, or even starting a full-time business.

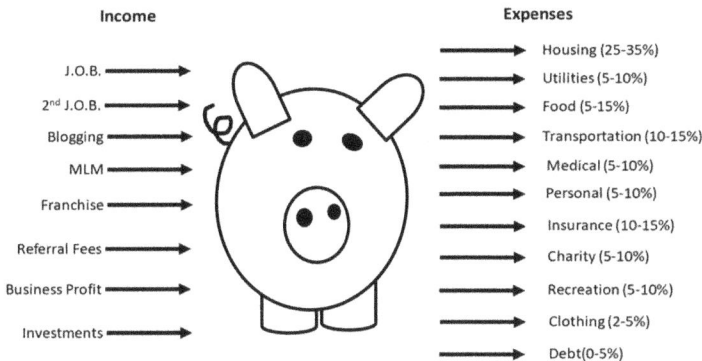

Figure 2 Feed the Pig

Imagine you have adjusted your income and expenses to the point where you can quit a job that you don't like and still keep the pig happily fed. How wonderful would that be? Perhaps you have realized that the second job fulfills your purpose and still provides enough income to keep the pig fed, so you quit your main job and start a business of your own in the field of the second job. Now you spend every day working on your purpose. How does that feel when you think about recreating your life this way? Are you excited? Are you nervous? It is your time—you get to decide how you will spend it.

The diagram below describes the three things that create your life and the choices on how to utilize them. The first of these three things is time.

You can choose to spend your time working toward making money by doing what gives your life joy. Or, you can choose to spend your time at a job you don't like, doing things that do not fulfill you, so you can pay your bills.

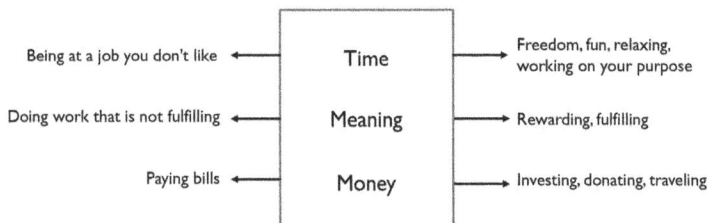

Figure 3   The 3 Elements That Create Your Life

What if you could shift your time, meaning, and money from the left side of this diagram to the right side? Would you feel as if your life were successful?

🌱 KEY POINT

Success is determined by whether you are devoting time to the activities you choose and the priorities in your life.

👣 ACTION STEPS

Watch the TED Talk: www.ted.com/talks/simon_sinek.

Ask yourself:

If I did not have to work to earn money, what else would I want to do with my time?

Write down your answer in your journal. If you come up with more than one activity, rank them in order of importance to you. Choose one small step you can imagine taking toward achieving that new activity.

Receiving Guidance

Tuning in to your favorite radio station may seem as simple as turning a dial or pushing a button, but there are several things going on behind the dials and buttons. The system is called a *Radio Frequency* (RF) *Receiver,* and its jobs are to receive signals, filter out all but the one you have chosen, and then send that one signal to the speakers so you can listen and enjoy the music. The first component in the system is an antenna that receives everything it possibly can receive. The antenna receives all the radio stations within broadcast range. The rest of the system tunes and filters and cleans, so all you hear is the one signal you chose. Without a functioning antenna, you will not receive anything.

It's the same when we ask for guidance in our lives. You must have a functioning antenna to receive, and to tune in, you must ask for guidance. There are many ways we can describe where we receive our guidance: Source, God, Universal Intelligence, the Divine, our Guides, the Angels. Whichever you choose, the guidance is always there; we only need to ask. Prayer is asking. To receive your guidance, simply sit still and listen (meditate). Prayer turns on your antenna and faith lets you receive the guidance.

Prayer means asking with your whole heart. You can pay attention to persistent thoughts afterward. These thoughts might be the answers you are looking for. Learn to relax and have faith that the answers will come. Each of us has a personal pattern of communicating with the Divine. Sometimes the answers come in dreams or as we are near deep sleep, so keep a note pad by your bed and write down significant messages you may receive as you awaken.

Be open to the answers you receive. They might not make sense immediately, but in time, their true meaning will be revealed. Ask once or twice and then wait for the answer. Ask for guidance and be open to unexpected answers. Your path is not always a straight line, and what you wish for might not be meant for you. This is why you should ask for guidance and not specific events or outcomes.

Say thank you when you receive the guidance. Be grateful to your Higher Power.

It is true that the guidance is always there for us, but our ability to receive that guidance depends on whether specific locations in our physical body, our mind, and energetic body (soul) are aligned and balanced. There are attributes that indicate whether these areas might be misaligned.

Deficient	Balanced	Excessive
Indecisive	Open to the Divine	Frustrated
Lacking creativity	Unafraid of death	Bipolar
Lacking intuition	Optimistic	Prone to migraines
Joyless	Looking for solutions	Slow to use personal power

Table 1   Is Your Ability to Receive Balanced?

The pineal gland is a small pinecone-shaped gland in the middle of the brain that acts like our RF receiver antenna. Although this gland is small, it is extremely powerful and essential. This is where we experience self-awareness and spiritual connection to Source. If you have ever had trouble sleeping for days, then you know what a dull and exhausted pineal gland feels like.

Receive Believe	Pineal Gland (crown chakra)
Open your mind to guidance and receive direction for your purpose.	
"Believe in your purpose"	

Figure 4 Receive and Believe

The pineal gland is extremely susceptible to fluoride deposits, which then block the ability to receive guidance. Since fluoride has been added to many public drinking water supplies (in an effort to reduce tooth decay) it is highly recommended that you filter any water that you consume with a filter that actually removes fluoride. Not all water filters remove fluoride.

Iodine can reduce the attraction of fluoride and other similar toxins into the endocrine system. But too much iodine can be harmful. Unless your doctor recommends supplements, you can achieve the appropriate level of iodine through food.

Listed below are things that will benefit your pineal gland for receiving guidance and things that you should avoid.

(+) 30 minutes of protected sunlight each day

(+) eating raw vegetables, especially green vegetables

(+) filtered water

(+) 7 to 9 hours of sleep daily in a dark, quiet environment

(-) Carbonated drinks

(-) Smog and environmental toxins

(-) Unfiltered or fluoridated water

(-) Irregular sleep, working third shift

Our bodies are in constant motion. Blood travels from the heart through the lungs and out to the arms and legs and then back again. Other fluids are moving through our lymphatic system. Electrical impulses continuously tell our heart to pump, the fluids to flow, tissue to grow, and toxins to release. This motion happens, yet we are barely aware that it does. We also might not be aware of the swirling areas of energy that are flowing within and around our physical body, but these centers of energy create the motion within our bodies.

The **Crown Chakra** is the energy center located around the pineal gland and at the top of the head. It resonates with the colors violet and white. It is the energetic body's antenna, and if it becomes off-balance, then your antenna will begin to feel either deficient or excessive and you will feel this imbalance in your ability to receive.

The mind is powerful. The act of simply believing something is true makes it true for you. By opening your mind to the possibility of receiving direction and guidance, asking for guidance, and awaiting that guidance, it becomes your truth. If you believe you will receive guidance, then you will.

By opening your mind to the possibility that you have an antenna with which you can receive guidance from Source, you are creating that ability. We all have that ability, but if you are not aware that it exists, you will not feel its presence.

So, close your eyes, and imagine a bright white light hovering just above your head. This white light represents your antenna. See it vibrating and glowing as it waits to connect with Source. Next, visualize a silver thread come down from heaven, and see it gently touch that white light. As the thread touches the light, see the white light become brighter yet. This silver thread represents *Source Knowledge* from God reaching down to you, connecting to your antenna, and feeding spiritual guidance into you through your antenna.

Then, speak these words to tune your mind to accept your ability to receive guidance from Source:

I am connected to my highest truth and guided by my inner wisdom.
As I speak, so shall it be.

You can take steps to help tune your crown chakra and improve the function of your RF antenna:

Color: The resonant colors of the crown chakra are violet and white. Focus on these colors. Find something with these colors and carry it with you to remind you to be open to receiving.

Vibration: The resonant frequency of the crown chakra is solfeggio 963 Hz, which is natural B, *Ti*. Listen to a solfeggio 963 Hz pure tone vibration (search for "963 tone crown chakra").

Sound: Listen to the wind, wind chimes, and tinkling bells.

Crystals: Tourmaline, white jade, diamond, clear quartz, selenite, and amethyst crystals help to balance the crown chakra. Set the crystal on the top of the head while you meditate.

Herbs/Essential Oils: Lavender, frankincense, sandalwood, and ginseng help to balance the crown chakra. Use the oil in a diffuser, or rub a drop or two on your hand, and smell the fragrance to remind you of your crown chakra.

Exercise: Imagine the top of your head is a funnel, and spiritual guidance is being poured into this funnel for you to live a successful and happy life.

Meditation/Prayer: Archangel Gabriel, *God's Messenger*. Ask him for guidance.

🌱 KEY POINT

When our pineal gland is healthy and resonating according to a healthy crown chakra energy center, it acts as a spiritual antenna, receiving guidance from Source.

👣 ACTION STEPS

Does your ability to receive guidance feel deficient, excessive, or balanced? In your journal, make a list of things you can do to improve your antenna. In the morning, meditate and pray before you get out of bed and ask Archangel Gabriel for guidance in the day ahead.

Accept

My Personal Navigation

Whether it was out of spite or selfishness, my ex-husband remained close with my family after I left him. My friends advised me that I needed to tell my family how much he had hurt me and how hard it had been for me to make the decision to leave. Up until that point, nobody knew; I was too ashamed of what had happened, and I was more ashamed that I had stayed. Only recently had I shared anything with even my closest friends.

Full of fear, I asked my family to meet with me.

My parents, my two closer brothers, and their wives were there. I was so nervous when I walked in because I was going to tell them I had endured treatment from my husband so similar to what I had endured as a child from them. I didn't have very high hopes that they would be supportive.

It was worse than I could have imagined.

My father told me that I had brought this man into the family, and that's where he would stay. My mother told me that if I wanted to leave, that was my choice. One of my brothers said it had been my choice to be a whore and shack up with some other guy. My other brother just laughed at me and said, "That's what you wanted to talk to us about?" And their wives just slumped in their chairs, one of them mouthing the words "I'm sorry" to me.

That was the day I decided to block my family from my life entirely. Their way of thinking had never aligned with what I wanted in my life. Although they should have been there to support me, they weren't. I wanted the wisdom to accept only what served my path. So, I chose to block the negativity of having them in my life.

This decision gave me a sense of freedom.

Since then, some things have improved between me and my family. I had continued to be very angry for years, until I finally chose to forgive—not for them, but for my own healing. I didn't forget and I kept the distance, but I needed to accept what was and release the hurt.

When I moved to Florida, it was much easier because there was a huge physical distance between us. Sometimes when I flew up to visit them, I was reminded that he was still part of the family. Pictures of his children on my mother's refrigerator were the most painful because, although I tried for years, I was never able to have children. It always felt like a slap across the face, a shock of reality around the truth of how much my family really didn't care about me.

During the plane ride home, I would look out the window and mentally throw all of that pain out and watch it drop to the earth and shatter.

Setting Healthy Boundaries

When my heart stopped beating, it was as if I stepped through a looking glass. I was aware, awake, and full of a bliss that cannot be adequately described. There were a million bright stars in a velvet blackness, a thickness and absence of everything except for the energy emanating from those stars that began to converge into a single bright light. I knew that each light was like a drop of water in a vast ocean of love. And they were all "talking" to me, singing to me together as if one harmonious voice. It was the cosmic consciousness. The bliss I felt was as if the purest of love energy was flowing through me, through the stars, and nothing else mattered except for this floating bliss. There was no fear, no sadness, and no pain. There was only love, carrying me across and cradling me in the softness of their loving arms. God's loving arms.

I "saw" all of this but without eyes, I "heard" but without ears, and I remembered something so deep and so ancient and so real, it pulled at my core.

Then, out of the ether, I heard: *It's not your time. You have to go back. You have work to do.*

Then I was back, back in my body, which felt heavy and odd, strange and disconnected. My senses were sharp and painful. Light and noise had a physical quality to them, piercing my brain. The smell of vomit in my hair penetrated and permeated my sinus cavity. Everything felt new, different, and painful. All of my senses hurt as if I were nothing but sunburned skin being submerged into hot water.

My physical body still looked the same, but inside, everything was different. Imagine trying to download iPhone software into an Android phone; my software was looking for something that wasn't there. My hardware wasn't being controlled at all. My bodily functions were going haywire, and I spent the next several weeks in the hospital and in bed, completely dependent on the wonderful nurses. It may seem like a horrible experience, but I was so full of love for everything and everybody that it was actually a beautiful emotional experience.

The most beautiful thing about experiencing the bliss of eternal consciousness and coming back into my physical form is that I returned with only love. I had gone with remnants of fear and sadness and even some anger and jealousy. Like an odor that stays on a shirt even after you wash it several times, I had been trying to wash these negative emotions out of my being for years.

And now, they were gone. My mind was free of regret. I held no grudges. I felt no fear. I had released the negative energies from the past, and I had remembered how to dance.

There are two ways you will know it is time to change—time to let go of the past, stop ruminating about what was and what might have been—and start living from where you are and toward what might become. The first is when you learn enough about yourself to know that you must change. The second is if you hit rock bottom, and you realize you have no option but to change. In my case, I had hit bottom.

If you know it is time to change, making the decision to change is still hard. For most of us, we have lived our entire lives thinking a certain way. Even if changing the way we live will be incredibly positive for us, it is the fear of change that keeps us from making changes, such as setting healthy boundaries. The fear that comes with the decision to change is not only about what the future might bring but also about what might happen if we simply say *no more* to the people in our lives who depend on us remaining the same.

Signs that you might be holding yourself back include:

- People tell you to calm down.

- It is difficult to hold a clear thought.

- You feel like you are in the wrong place, like you don't belong.

- You feel like you need to be doing something different with your life.

- You get irritated easily.

- You have a constant feeling of dread.

Before I became so sick, I had all these signs on top of feeling like someone was screaming in my head: *You are not living the life you were meant to live!* I tried to make the changes I knew I needed to make, but making some of these changes would mean that the lives of people in my life would also change and perhaps not the way they might like. When I started talking about making changes in my life, I received a fair amount of pushback from the people who depended on me remaining the same. And I wasn't clear enough about who I was to know I must change.

Since I didn't make the changes for myself, the Universe made them for me. My heart stopped beating and I flatlined. It was my rock-bottom moment.

A boundary is a line that may not be crossed. A fence is a boundary. A point in time can be a boundary. Borders are boundaries. You have personal boundaries. Remember that because they are personal to you, others may not recognize them and may do something that crosses your personal boundaries. You must tell people what your boundaries are and when they are close to crossing them or bumping up against them.

If you have been feeling the need to make changes in the boundaries in your life, and you have decided it is time to make those changes, then it is your responsibility to vocalize these boundaries to others. It is up to you to decide what your personal boundaries are, set them clearly, and disclose these boundaries to the people in your life. Disclose the boundaries so that the people in your life understand clearly what your personal boundaries are. If they do not respect those boundaries, you may take decisive action, knowing that at least you have information about that relationship.

🌱 KEY POINT

When you realize that part of your life must change, you can no longer pretend you don't know it.

👣 ACTION STEPS

What areas of your life cause you stress? Ask yourself if they feel aligned with your true self. If they do not feel aligned, ask yourself what needs to change. Record your ideas and insights in your journal.

Thinking Your Own Thoughts

Before I flatlined, I wasn't clear about my boundaries. They weren't clear to me, so there was no way I could make them clear to anyone else. It was difficult for me to hold a clear thought about anything that had to do with myself. I was so afraid that if I vocalized any boundaries to my loved ones, they might not respect those boundaries, and that rejection would be too much to bear. The bottom line was that I didn't believe that my needs mattered, so I didn't speak up for what I needed or wanted.

I knew that I had to change. As time passed, a deep feeling of fear began to build—fear of a reckoning day when I would finally stand up for myself, my loved ones would reject me, and then I would be alone. Because I was afraid, I began noticing circumstances around me that crossed my personal boundaries. These may have never bothered me before, but suddenly, emotions were racing through me, emotions of anger and resentment. I became irritable with my husband, and of course, he was irritable to me in return. All of this reinforced the belief that I wasn't worthy of his love and respect. It was a crazy cycle, and as much as I tried to understand and rationalize the situation, I couldn't. I was stuck.

This is how fear creates roadblocks in our lives: A circumstance causes us to **believe** something bad may happen. Once we believe it, we think it—*something bad will happen*—and that **thought** stays with us. The more we **connect** with that thought, the more it **resonates** throughout the day and in any situation. Now with that fear resonating with all we do, it becomes the **focus**. We watch for something bad to happen; we expect it. We focus on what might be bad and emphasize when negative things happen, reinforcing the **belief**.

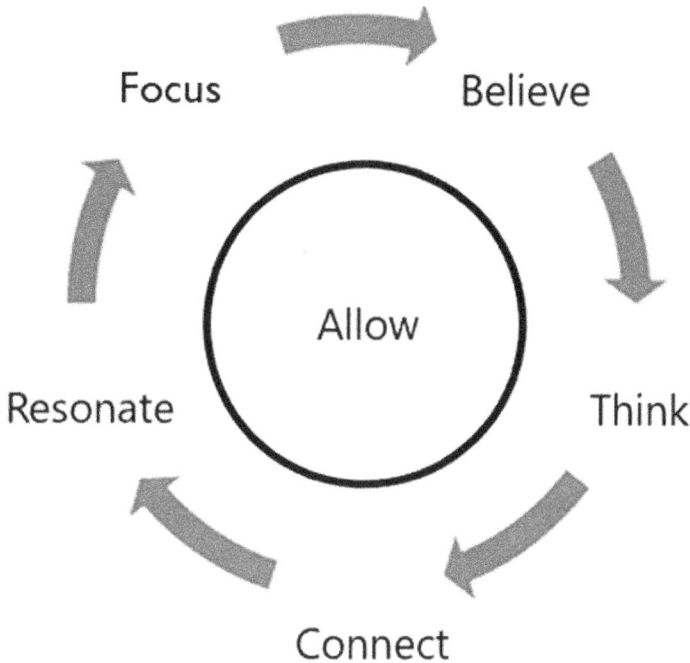

Figure 5 How to Change Your Life

It's hard to change our beliefs because they become hardwired into our brains. Sometimes this happens at a very young age, and sometimes it happens because we experience trauma as an adult. If we can change one part of this cycle, then we, ourselves, can change. We humans are the only species on the planet that can think about what we think. If we can change our thoughts, then we can break the cycle, and our feelings will change, which will change our emotions. If we can change our emotion of fear to a different emotion, like excitement, that will enable us to take action, and then we will no longer be stuck.

As humans, because of the way our brains have evolved, we are able to think about our thoughts and change them in order to break this cycle. The table below shows the three types of brains. Cold-blooded animals have only the reptilian brain. Warm-blooded birds and animals have both the reptilian brain and the *paleomammalian brain*. Humans have three brains: the reptilian brain, the paleomammalian brain, and the *neomammalian brain*.

	Reptilian Brain	Paleomammalian Brain	Neomammalian Brain
Primary Function	Regulates the body and generates immediate survival responses	Creates and connects basic emotions to memories and vocal communication	Processes information directly from the rest of the brain, using sophisticated reasoning
Characteristics	Generates the fight/flight responses, shifting blood flow from the cerebral cortex for fast physical reaction and immediate survival	Generates basic emotions (anger, sadness, happiness, fear) and provides a sense of self and the ability to feel empathy	Allows us to learn complex concepts, reason about our experiences, and develop a moral framework (belief in a higher being)

Table 2   The Human Brain

The reptilian brain consists of the brain stem and only the parts of the brain necessary for regulating the body's immediate survival responses. It is the body's alarm system that prepares the body to either fight, flight (*Run away!*) or freeze (*If I don't move, then the danger will pass* *by without seeing me*). When this alarm goes off, the hypothalamic/pituitary/adrenal systems send signals to the parasympathetic nervous system to flood the body with hormones in order to speed up the heart rate and quicken respiration in preparation for fight or flight. Too much of this causes us to freeze in place, frozen with fear.

The paleomammalian brain consists of the layer above the reptilian brain. This is where emotions are generated as we make connections between what is happening in our world and how we feel about what is happening in the world. Our memories are created here, and emotions are attached to those memories.

The neomammalian brain is the outer-most layer of our brain, above the paleomammalian brain. This is the part of the brain that makes us human. We are lucky to be human because we have the processing part of the brain that enables us to *think about thinking*. This enables us to think about how we can shift our thoughts to change our results. Although other mammals can create memories and attach emotions to those memories, we are the only species on Earth who can think about what those emotions regarding memories mean and imagine thinking differently about those memories. We are able to reason. We can learn complex concepts, understand what time means, and believe in a Source/God.

🌱 KEY POINT

Humans can think about their thoughts. Therefore, they can change their thoughts in order to change their feelings.

👣 ACTION STEPS

Think about something that has been causing you to feel stressed lately. Listen to the actual words your mind speaks to you. Write them down in your journal. The action of listening to your thoughts is proof that you can think about what you are thinking about.

Now create a different stream of words for your mind to speak. Write them down too. Force your mind to speak these new words. Notice how your feelings change.

Shielding Yourself From Negative Energy

Although energy cannot be seen with the physical eye, it is real and flows from person to person. There may have been a time or two when you have walked into a room, and without having heard the argument or seen sour looks between two people, you could feel the anger in the energy of the room. Once this energy attaches to you, it does not let go until you clear it from your energetic body or replace it with good energy. If you do not clear it or replace it, then it might hold you back by affecting your ability to receive and use your guidance in a healthy way.

Signs there is negative energy that could be holding you back:

- Hypervigilance
- Not being able to let go of emotions
- Constant complaining
- Interactions with people become difficult
- Persistent feelings of anxiety
- Frequently seeking isolation
- Low self-esteem
- Feeling on edge or angry
- Critical of self and others
- Chronic negativity

Improving Your Ability to Release What Doesn't Serve You

When negative feelings, such as guilt, shame, sadness, frustration, anger, and fear are experienced but you deny your body the ability to process those feelings, the feelings get stuck. If there are emotions trapped within the body, they block other emotions that also want to flow. Imagine that anger is a big boulder, and it gets stuck in the stream of your energetic body. You might think you are doing the right thing by not showing your anger, but you have blocked the flow of other emotions. Suppose there is grief inside you that needs to be felt to be released—if a boulder of anger is blocking the flow, how can you grieve? Neither can you feel deep joy. It's impossible to connect authentically with others if you are going through life with only the masks of emotions.

There are healthy ways to let your emotions come up and flow through you. It takes practice, but the first step is releasing the emotions that are stuck because keeping them blocked inside is holding you back.

When you release negative emotions, it does not mean you forget the memories associated with those emotions. We are always defined by our memories, but the limiting beliefs associated with our memories can be released if the emotions associated with the memories can flow through us. You can let go of the limiting beliefs that control your thoughts, feelings, emotions, actions, and results. By letting go—releasing the beliefs and thoughts around the feelings—you can release the feelings, too, and you will be set free.

Guidance is always available to us, but our ability to receive that guidance depends on whether specific locations in our physical body, our mind, and energetic body (soul) are aligned and balanced. There are attributes that indicate whether these areas might be misaligned.

Deficient	Balanced	Excessive
Undisciplined	Nonmaterialistic	Egotistical
Meek	Charismatic	Arrogant
Indifferent	Inquisitive	Manipulative
Oversensitive	Respectful	Condescending

Table 3   How Balanced Is Your Ability to Think and Accept?

The **Third Eye Chakra** acts like a filter, blocking things that are not important for us to focus on so that we can direct our attention more appropriately. It is associated with the pituitary gland, which is a small pinecone-shaped gland located directly in the center of your brain between your ears and between your eyes. The third eye gives us the wisdom to think clearly. If we were to focus on everything all the time, we would be overloaded with information and unable to think clearly about anything.

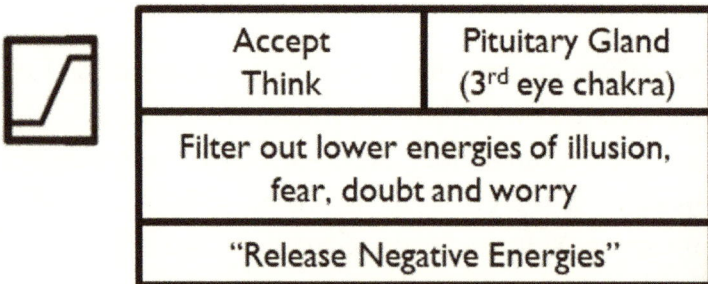

Accept Think	Pituitary Gland (3rd eye chakra)
Filter out lower energies of illusion, fear, doubt and worry	
"Release Negative Energies"	

Figure 6   Accept and Think

The pituitary gland helps regulate the function of all the endocrine glands. It is the thermostat of all the endocrine functions, maintaining *homeostasis* or a state of equilibrium in which fluids and endocrine function are flowing and balanced.

Nutritional support for the third eye chakra includes:

- **High-protein foods,** high in amino acids, enable the pituitary gland to release hormones, particularly the human growth hormone. A protein is a chain of amino acids connected together. Our endocrine system turns amino acids into amino acid derivatives, called *hormones*, which are stored in endocrine cells until needed. High-protein foods do not cause the release, but they do make hormone release possible. In other words, we must eat protein-rich foods for the pituitary to release hormones. Amino acids are the building blocks of our bodies and are found in good protein sources like lean beef, fish, poultry, nuts, and eggs. If you are a vegetarian or vegan, you must find a way to add amino acids to your diet.

- **Manganese** is required for proper pituitary function. It is found in leafy greens, nuts, legumes, and whole grains.

- **Vitamin E** protects the pituitary gland from free radicals. Foods high in vitamin E include wheat germ, nuts, sunflower seeds, almonds, salmon, trout, and avocado.

- **Vitamin D** helps the pituitary gland to secrete hormones. The main way to get vitamin D is via direct sunlight. Foods that contain vitamin D include fatty fish, fortified milk, beef liver, cheese, and egg yolk.

By opening your mind to the possibility of releasing negativity so that you can move forward, you are creating that reality, and it shall be so. For centuries and through many religions and cultures, this location has been known to be the center of wisdom. Focusing on the center of your forehead with your eyes closed can help you to tune your mind to expand your insight and your ability to sense what is around you. I practice using my third eye when I am doing things like clasping my necklace behind my neck. I close my eyes and imagine that I am seeing what my hands are doing. I close my eyes and place my attention to that location in the center of my forehead and then to the back of my neck where my fingers are holding the clasp, and it is done. Try it. It takes practice, but you will build the ability to see things without using physical sight.

Speak these words and tune your mind to accept your ability to release negative thoughts and trust in your intuitive knowledge:

I am fully grounded and supported with a healthy energy flow.
As I speak, so shall it be.

The **Third Eye Chakra** is the energy center located around the pituitary gland. It resonates with a deep blue color. If it becomes imbalanced, then you will begin to feel either deficient or excessive, and you will feel this imbalance in your ability to release.

You can take steps to tune your third eye chakra:

Color: The resonant color of the third eye chakra is deep blue. Focus on this color. Find something with this color, and carry it with you to remind you to focus.

Vibration: The resonant frequency of the third eye chakra is solfeggio 852 Hz, which is natural A, *La*. Listen to a solfeggio 852 Hz pure tone vibration (search Google for "852 tone third eye chakra").

Sound: Listen to deeper-toned wind chimes or wind instruments, like the flute.

Crystals: Amethyst, sugilite, lapis. Set the crystals on your forehead head while you meditate.

Herbs/Essential Oils: Frankincense, myrrh, and patchouli herbs help to tune the third eye chakra. Use the oil in a diffuser or rub a drop or two on your hand and smell the fragrance to remind you of your third eye chakra.

Foods: Blueberries, blackberries, raisins, eggplant, caffeine, organic chocolate, red wine, mint tea, organic apple cider.

Exercise: Close your eyes and picture a white light in the middle of your forehead. This is your third eye.

Meditation/Prayer: Archangel Michael, *He Who Is Like God.* Ask him to help you filter out lower energies of illusion and doubt.

🌱 KEY POINT

When your pituitary gland is healthy and resonating according to a healthy third eye chakra energy center, it acts as a spiritual high-pass filter, allowing you to think clearly and receive Source guidance clearly.

👣 ACTION STEPS

Is it difficult to allow positive thoughts into your mind? Are you feeling deficient or excessive in third eye chakra energy? In your journal, make a list of things you can do to improve your ability to allow. Ask Archangel Michael to help you filter out lower energies of illusion and doubt

Release

My Personal Navigation

When I awoke from my first 528Hz meditation, I was fully present. As I sat up, I realized how calm everything felt, how clear it all was. I looked down at the floor, and for the first time, I saw the patterns in the hardwood. It wasn't that I didn't know they had been there; it was more that I hadn't seen them. I looked at my hands and connected to the life that was flowing within them, recognizing them as part of my body, part of me, rather than appendages that I used to manipulate items around me. I saw flickering shadows on the walls, smelled something fresh and sweet—the apples on the counter. I was alone and the silence was audible, deafening. Instead of only being aware of the incessant ramblings of my worried mind, I heard . . . nothing. And yet I knew everything.

I was in the space between what was and what could be.

It is in this place that clarity exists. It is where truth reveals itself.

I hung in that space, like an astronaut floating untethered. Even as I stood to look in the mirror and feel both of us, Gabriel and me, looking at my face, I hung in that space between. It was what some spiritual teachers call The Gap.

That entire year with Gabriel I stayed in the gap. It was natural for him to exist there, and I gladly followed his lead. He gave me the gift of knowing what it was like to live there in that space between. But Gabriel left me when I flatlined, and I returned to this physical realm like a pilot, trying to fly solo for the first time. I sometimes found myself swirling between worry and fear, and like a new pilot, I searched my memory for a solution.

Connecting to ground and remembering previous times I was able to get centered always helped. I love to garden for that very reason. The first time

I became completely and fully aware of the moment while gardening, my hands had been deep into the warm earth, planting peppers. Suddenly, everything in my sight came into full focus. The colors were vivid and bright without blinding me, like a camera that can focus close and far away at the same time; it all became clear. The different greens of the grass, the palmettos, the palm fronds, the leaves on the trees, and the colors were as different to me as black is to white. My hearing opened as if both ears popped at once, revealing to me the sound the wind made, the branches scraping against one another, sounds that were hidden to me until then. It wasn't that I couldn't hear these things before that; instead, it was as if everything had been muffled. I hadn't been paying attention because I was worried about things that happened a moment or more ago, and I was fearful of what might happen in the moments ahead. The moment I had wasn't even being experienced.

The Woman in the Mirror

Research has shown that self-esteem develops and matures until about the age of five,[2] and although throughout your life your self-esteem may wax and wane, the way you think about yourself is pretty much complete by age nine.[3]

A famous psychologist, Erik Erikson, theorized that a healthy sense of self as an adult depends on successfully developing psychosocially at specific stages of your life. Failure to complete a stage will leave you

2 Cvencek, Dario, et al. "Implicit Measures for Preschool Children Confirm Self-Esteem's Role in Maintaining a Balanced Identity." *Journal of Experimental Social Psychology* 62 50–57. 2016. ilabs.washington.edu
3 Robins, Richard W. and Kali H. Trzesniewski. "Self-Esteem Development Across the Lifespan" *Current Directions in Psychological Science.* 14:3 158–162. 2005. doi.org/10.1111/j.0963-7214.2005.00353.x

unable to emerge from that level. You will be left with an inadequate sense of self to continue to the next stage.[4]

I was taught that I didn't matter—that I was dirty, worthless, a disgrace to the family. I regularly heard the words: *Who the hell do you think you are?* and *You're nothing special.* Yet at the same time, I was told that the only people who would ever be there for me was my family. So, I wore my masks and went through life hiding, working hard, and not shining too brightly.

Some believe that every time you experience something extremely painful, a piece of your soul becomes stuck in that experience. The rest of your being continues to move forward in time, but incomplete. Before my NDE, there were many times I felt this way—like a shell, catatonic and incomplete.

When I flatlined and then returned to my body as a clear and whole spiritual being without any emotional attachments to painful memories, everything was different. I was completely and authentically myself. But the problem was that my body didn't have the physical construct to support this clarity. Inside I knew who I was, and I didn't feel the need to be anything different for anyone. I felt complete and authentic. But I also felt unable to interact with the world. I couldn't wear my masks anymore, and I couldn't *not* wear them. I felt stiff. I could physically talk, but I couldn't describe or explain how I felt or why I felt that way. It is the difference between saying you want meatloaf for dinner and explaining why you like meatloaf. There is a difference. I was a stranger in a strange body.

After I began recovering, I realized the disconnect, and I started working with different coaches to build the neurological connections required to physically interact and react according to my authentic

4 Cherry, Kendra. "Erik Erikson's Stages of Psychosocial Development." 2019. verywellmind.com/erik-eriksons-stages-of-psychosocial-development-2795740

self. One of the most healing exercises included connecting to my inner child. This was important because this was who I was when my healthy sense of self would have developed and when the bridge had not been completed. I would mentally reach out to my younger self in my mind to hug her, to make her laugh and feel safe to be herself; but she was wary of me just like she had been wary of everyone when she was little. She would stay just out of sight, around the doorway, and behind the wall. I could feel her there, standing silent and motionless, her little hands clasped behind her back. She didn't trust me. It took months of just being with her and being there for her, and finally, she showed her little face to me. It took several more months for the little girl inside of me to let the grown woman "me" hug her. This was powerful integration. I shed many tears, hugging myself and visualizing I was hugging that incredibly misunderstood, scared, and hurt little child.

Other exercises that really helped me understand my true self explored the masks I had worn throughout my life and why I wore them. We each have an identity we choose to show to others. If we are integrated and emotionally healthy, then we do that authentically. Up until my NDE, I spent my life in full protection mode, strategizing and planning for the inevitable crisis. My mask was that of a woman in total control of every aspect of her life, not letting anyone else get in too close so she wouldn't get hurt—willing to do whatever it takes to not need anyone for anything too important.

Now, when I refer back to my writing about the mask I wore, it makes me want to cry. I had so much protection up, it is a wonder I felt anything. Maybe I didn't.

Another reason I know my illness is a blessing is because I am human now.

We all wear some kind of mask. My mask was one of stone. Yours may not be as drastic. Some of us wear more than one mask, depending on whom we are with and what the situation is. The mask depends on how we want to be perceived by others, but the fact is that a mask cannot hide everything about you. The mask you choose will still reflect some of the truth within. So, reflecting on the way you choose to be seen is a great place to start when you feel that you are not being truly authentic.

🌱 KEY POINT

When you experience something extremely painful in your life, it affects you in many ways.

👣 ACTION STEPS

What painful experiences have you had, and what age were you when you experienced them? Note in your journal what you remember.

Find a photograph of yourself at that age and look deeply into your eyes. What comes up for you?

Imagine that you are hugging yourself at that time. Hold yourself closely and give yourself comfort. Tell yourself that it is okay to cry, and it is okay to let go of the pain. What supportive and loving message do you wish you had at the time? Write that message to yourself now in your journal.

Who Am I?

Sometimes people have difficulty connecting with who they are, especially after having been through trauma, abuse, or simply living their entire lives for others, never considering their own wants or needs. They become disillusioned that there was any purpose for the path they had taken and are not sure which direction is best for them to follow in the future.

When someone is faced with this dilemma, it is sometimes easiest to start with what they know to be true. To help people begin to look inward for a starting point of self-identity, I like two methods: *Enneagrams* and *archetypes*. Go to GeriBurke.com/Enneagram to take the Enneagram quiz and determine which Enneagram you identify with the most. Go to GeriBurke.com/archetype and take the archetype quiz to see which of the archetypes is closest to your personality. You will receive personalized reports with the results for each quiz.

Enneagrams

An Enneagram is a tool used to describe how someone relates to self, others, and the world. There are nine distinct Enneagram types, each describing different inter-personality dynamics. In other words, your Enneagram describes how you typically interact with other Enneagrams. By understanding which type you most closely identify with, you can better understand and accept why you choose to do some of the things that you do. This is not to say that you submit to the weaknesses of the Enneagram, but rather to understand what those weaknesses, as well as the strengths, are. If you are aware of what areas could be troublesome in your life, you are more able to change that behavior when it arises.

Enneagram	Typical Methods of Interacting
The Reformer	Purposeful, self-controlled, perfectionist
The Helper	Generous, people-pleasing
The Achiever	Driven, image-conscious, adaptable
The Individualist	Dramatic, expressive, temperamental

The Investigator	Innovative, perceptive, isolated
The Loyalist	Responsible, engaging, anxious
The Enthusiast	Spontaneous, scattered, flexible
The Challenger	Self-confident, willful, confrontational
The Peacemaker	Receptive, reassuring, resigned

Table 4   How Do You Interact With Others?

Archetypes

Archetypes are another personality model, but instead of being based on how you interact with others, your archetype describes a recurrent behavior you have been exhibiting in your life. The premise is that you will live your life based on your archetype even if you are not aware that you are doing so. There are twelve archetypes.

Archetype	Recurrent Behavior Pattern
The Innocent	Optimistic, finds silver linings
The Orphan	Cynical, looks for a place to fit in
The Hero	Courageous, shows their strength
The Caregiver	Empathic, helps others
The Seeker	Wondering, seeks new experiences
The Rebel	Revolutionary, makes change
The Lover	Committed, pleases others
The Creator	Visionary, does things differently
The Jester	Comedic, lightens the mood
The Sage	Thinking, contemplates the world

| The Magician | Inventive, makes dreams come true |
| The Ruler | Guiding, improves community |

Table 5 What Is Your Behavior Pattern?

These are just two methods of looking at your inner self and your intrinsic value. They typically shed light on why you are drawn to certain types of work and react in certain ways when dealing with other people. These are neither good nor bad. Each Enneagram and archetype has its own strengths and weaknesses, just as we each have our own.

One of my clients was frustrated with the path she had taken in her career. She was a speech therapist, working with stroke victims, helping them learn to speak clearly again. But she felt like she had chosen this path at random, and something important was missing. And, she was not making enough money for the number of hours she was spending. She was always exhausted. When she took the Enneagram and archetype quizzes, she realized the importance of the choices she had made. Her Enneagram was The Helper and her archetype was The Caregiver. She realized the work she was doing supported both the ways she interacted with others and the way she truly felt inside. But she was still not happy with the number of hours she was putting in and the amount of pay she received.

So, we redesigned her career, adjusting the way she was coaching speech, so that she would have more income and feel more fulfilled. We used her background to create a business to help small businesses communicate clearly about their business and deliver presentations that connected with their audiences. She has now more than doubled her income and is working fewer than twenty hours a week, speaking to groups around the world and coaching from her home office.

🌱 KEY POINT

People who have been through traumatic experiences can use methods like the Enneagrams and the archetypes to help them begin to identify with their strengths and value.

👣 ACTION STEPS

Go to my website, GeriBurke.com/Enneagram, and take the Enneagram quiz to determine which Enneagram you most identify with. You will receive a personalized report with the results of your quiz. Journal about which Enneagram you have identified with and how you feel about that choice. Is there a different Enneagram that you would have preferred? Which one? Why?

Go to my website, GeriBurke.com/archetype, to take the Archetype quiz and see which of the archetypes is closest to your personality. You will receive a personalized report with the results of your quiz. Journal about which archetype you were identified with and how you feel about that choice. Is there a different archetype that you would have preferred? Which one? Why?

Release Negative Energy and Be Yourself

At each stage of our life, we can look back to see how far we have come. When we look at our current life as a culmination of our past experiences, we can understand what experiences we have integrated into who we are and what challenges have given us the perspectives and strengths we have today.

At the end of the film, *The Wizard of Oz*, the good witch Glinda tells Dorothy that she always had the power to grant her own wish, but she needed to learn it for herself to believe it. It is not about where you have been; it is about who you have become. And it requires that you see yourself for all that you are. You must embrace the glorious and beautiful mess you have become.

Are you ready to see yourself? Are you ready to connect with the truth?

Are you ready to just *be yourself?*

We tend to *do* too much and *be* too little—as if the energy we expend is itself achievement—and by doing so, we increase our feelings of worth and value. But our true self is who we are when we let go of the stories that make us think we need to *do* more in order to *be* more.

We are enough.

The guidance is always there for us to just be ourselves, but our ability to receive that guidance depends on whether specific locations in our physical body, our mind, and energetic body are aligned and balanced. There are attributes that indicate whether these areas might be misaligned.

Deficient	Balanced	Excessive
Daydreaming	Possessing self-mastery	Dominating
Lacking sex drive	Leading healthy sex life	Focusing on genitals
Procrastinating	Manifesting abundance	Materialistic
Lacking self-esteem	Possessing healthy self-esteem	Selfish

Table 6   How Balanced Is Your Ability to be Present?

The **Root Chakra** is the energy center that is associated with the *adrenal glands* and is located at the base of your spine. The adrenal glands are attached to the top of your kidneys. The root chakra is like the roots of a tree; the deeper and stronger your root chakra is, the more you are able to be in the moment. The moment is the only true reality and the only place you have any real control. The past is gone. It's wise to contemplate lessons learned, so you do not repeat mistakes, but dwelling on what is gone does not serve you. The future is not yet here, and although you can plan for the future, if you spend all of your time worrying about what might happen, you miss out on all that is happening.

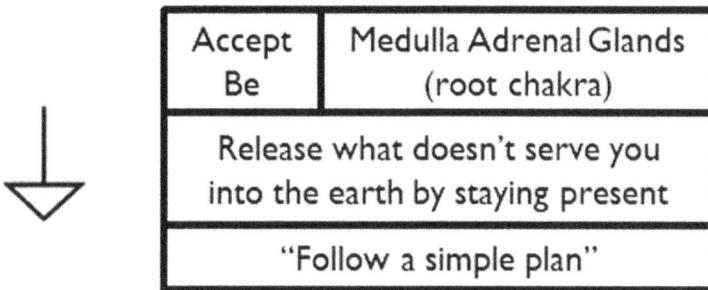

Accept Be	Medulla Adrenal Glands (root chakra)
	Release what doesn't serve you into the earth by staying present
	"Follow a simple plan"

Figure 7   Accept and Be

The adrenal glands control essential bodily functions by producing hormones that help regulate metabolism, the immune system, and blood pressure, in addition to controlling your response to stress by releasing epinephrine and cortisol.

To keep your body's grounding system healthy, prevent stress as much as you can. And when you cannot prevent stress, give your body the downtime it needs to recover.

Some strategies to keep your adrenals healthy:

- Get seven to nine hours of uninterrupted sleep each night.

- Eat a light meal every two to four hours, but not within two hours of bedtime.

- Exercise ten to thirty minutes three to five times per week.

- Connect with Source through prayer and meditation.

- Stay connected with others; keep in touch with your friends.

- Be realistic with your to-do list and build breaks into your day.

- Get outside and connect with nature for ten to fifteen minutes each day.[5]

- Stay connected to yourself and your emotions through journaling.

By opening your mind to the possibility of releasing negativity so that you can move forward, you cause the negativity to release. The root chakra is what provides you the gift of being in your physical body. If your thoughts drift off and you forget where you are, then you know how it feels when your root chakra weakens. It is sometimes nice to daydream. While meditating, I let my root chakra relax deeply so that my consciousness can travel outside my body. But while I am in my body and engaging with the physical world, it is helpful to have my root chakra completely engaged and secure, having released all negative energies. This is called being *well-grounded*.

Speak these words and tune your mind to release negative thoughts and trust in your intuitive knowledge:

---

5 **Note:** Every electronic device must connect to a lower voltage in order to release the signals it filters out. The earth has the lowest voltage in the physical realm. In order to physically release the low-frequency vibrations we pick up all day, we must physically connect to the earth. The fastest and easiest way to send them to the earth is to physically touch the earth or a tree or the grass with our naked skin.

I am free from fear.
Any unwanted energies are drained away from me.
As I speak, so shall it be.

The **Root Chakra** is the energy center that is located around the adrenal glands. It resonates with the color red. If it becomes off-balance, then you will begin to feel either deficient or excessive, and you will feel this imbalance in your ability to feel present and in the moment.

You can tune your root chakra in many ways:

Color: The resonant color of the root chakra is red. Focus on this color. Find something with this color, and carry it with you to remind you to focus.

Vibration: The resonant frequency of the root chakra is solfeggio 396 Hz, which is natural C, or Do. Listen to a solfeggio 396 Hz pure tone vibration (search Google for "396 tone root chakra").

Sound: Beat on drums and listen to chanting; listen to deep base instruments such as drums, cello, and tuba.

Crystals: Hematite, black tourmaline, red jasper, garnet, ruby, bloodstone. Set the crystals at the base of the spine while you meditate.

Herbs/Essential Oils: Ylang-Ylang, cedar atlas, juniper, and cinnamon are herbs that help to tune the root chakra. Use the oil in a diffuser or rub a drop or two on your hand and smell the fragrance to remind you of your root chakra.

Exercises: Walk barefoot in the grass, hug a tree, sit on the ground outside and breathe the air.

Meditation/Prayer: Archangel Uriel, *God's Light*. Ask him to help you stay present and grounded to Mother Earth.

🌱 KEY POINT

When your adrenal glands are healthy and resonating according to a healthy root chakra energy center, they act as a spiritual grounding, allowing you to release negativity into the Earth, to be in the present moment, and to be who you are completely.

👣 ACTION STEPS

The absolute best way to improve the vibration and health of your adrenal glands is to get closer to the Earth. If it is warm enough outdoors, walk barefoot in the grass. Hug a tree, and as you hold onto the trunk, look up at the branches. As tall as the branches go, the roots go down. Imagine any negative thoughts and feelings being drawn down along those roots and into the depths of the Earth. Feel how strong the tree is and how protected you are just by holding on.

Ask Archangel Uriel to help keep you focus on the present moment and connect to Mother Earth.

Connect

My Personal Navigation

I started getting sick several years before my NDE. My entire airway felt sick. My voice was always raspy, and I went through bouts of laryngitis anytime I caught the slightest cold. I would get the sensation that my throat was being squeezed, especially on the sides of my neck. The pressure on my carotid arteries made it feel like I wasn't getting enough oxygen to my brain. The doctors checked to make sure that there were no blockages in those arteries, and there weren't, but it felt like there were.

Looking back on all my symptoms, I realize that it was probably my vagus nerve, causing most of the issues. The vagus nerve is the tenth cranial nerve, also called "the traveling nerve" because it branches into two after leaving the brain and then travels down both sides of the neck right next to each carotid artery, touches your throat, and then continues down through the body, innervating with every organ in the body. It's part of the autonomic nervous system, helping your body to react to fear so you can escape danger.

My voice and throat were really affected. I couldn't speak my truth. I didn't know what my truth was. I wasn't connected to other people, nor was I connected to myself or even the present moment. There was something inside me that was urging me to wake up and engage, but I was full of fear.

I would go to meetings, and I would be thinking about what I was going to say—what could I say? Was it the right thing to say? Was it the right time to say it? And then after I did say something, I would be worried if I said it the right way. Did they want to hear what I said? Did they care about what I said? Are they upset with me for saying what I said?

Crazy! What I put myself through was crazy!

Being with Gabriel helped a lot. I lived through him. I felt what it was like to be normal. It was a glorious year of my life.

But I was still having trouble with my throat. Once, the doctor needed to take a swab of my throat to check for strep, and she warned me that it would make me gag. But I didn't gag. She was surprised, and I told her that I don't have a gag reflex. She did it again, and still, I didn't gag. It was funny at the time, but looking back, it was a sign that something wasn't right with my vagal nerve. I had no idea. The doctor had no idea.

It amazes me when I look back and realize how many signs there were right there in front of my doctors. They just kept looking in their own little specialty box and finding nothing wrong.

After my NDE, it was as if my entire vagal nerve had been hit by lightning. My heart had stopped and then started, and in the process, my entire nervous system had been reset. It left me unable to swallow without gagging, and my right vocal cord was paralyzed. My ability to connect deeply and honestly with others had been shocked into life, but I first needed to learn how to use this newly awakened part of my body.

A Successful Life

I ran away from home several times before the age of eighteen. When I graduated from high school, I left my family for good. I studied drafting and worked toward a ten-month certification. At first, I was homeless, sometimes sleeping on the couch of a fellow student. Then I worked at McDonald's for a few months, and then finally I went on welfare. I knew that there would come a day when I would pay every cent back into the system, but I still felt so embarrassed when I bought food with the food stamp coupons. This was in 1980, and subsidized food was purchased with paper coupons before the welfare system used cards.

Every week I would buy a bag of apples, a jar of peanut butter, and a loaf of bread. I carried them in my bookbag and sat alone while I ate. It sounds like a sad time, but I was happy because I felt safe. When I graduated and got my first job and my first paycheck, I knew what it meant to feel secure.

When I was twenty-one, I married a man I thought was my best friend. I loved him very much, and I knew that he loved me too. But, on our first anniversary, he punched through the front window of our house out of frustration and anger. Like a good wife, I swept up the glass and wiped up the blood. And then I pushed what happened back into the recesses of my mind, just like I had throughout my childhood.

How easily I had become a shell of a person—again.

Three years later, in a fit of jealous rage, he punched me so hard in the chest that he fractured my sternum. Then as I gasped for breath, he pushed me down on the dining room floor and raped me violently.

And still, I stayed with him.

Another four years passed, with me giving in to his every desire, denying myself everything, including a thought of my own. I had completely withdrawn—again.

One night, he woke me by ripping off my clothes. He grabbed me by my throat with his left hand and slammed me against the wall, his right hand clenched in a fist, ready to strike me in the face. This time when I cried out, he let me go, and I ran to the bathroom and locked the door. And that is where I awoke the next morning, naked and shivering on the tile floor. At first, I didn't know where I was, but as I stood, I remembered everything. When I looked in the mirror, the sight of me caused such a shock that I awoke from the depths of my mind.

How had my life come to this again?

In that moment, cold and naked, hair matted to my face from the tears, I saw myself clearly for the first time in my life. It was as if everything shifted, even the sunlight streaming in the bathroom window got brighter. Something deep within my ears cleared, and I could hear more clearly. I looked in the mirror and saw my face; I looked into my eyes and saw . . . *myself*. And I cried for myself and for all the pain I had lived with for my entire life.

At that moment, I knew I had wanted to belong so badly that I had sacrificed my security. I knew I needed to re-create my life.

I promised myself: *I will never let anyone ever hurt me again.*

I promised myself: *I will always take care of myself and never again feel like I need someone else so much that I lose myself in the process.*

I promised myself: *No matter how long it takes, I will heal from all that I have been through.*

That was the beginning of my healing journey.

In 1943, Abraham Maslow published the paper "A Theory of Human Motivation,"[6] which describes the stages of the development of human needs:

- At the basic physiological level, we all need to **survive**; we all need food, oxygen, water, and warmth.

- After the need to survive is fulfilled, we can then focus on the need to simply **feel safe and secure**, the freedom from feeling fearful.

---

6 Maslow, A. H. "A Theory of Human Motivation." Originally published in *Psychological Review*, 50:4, 370–396. 1943. doi:10.1037/h0054346

- After there is not an immediate fear to focus on, we can turn our attention to the need for **human relationships** (family, friends, lovers).

- When the need for relationships has been met, we turn to **achieving recognition** to earn the respect of others.

This is the point at which most people think the pinnacle of success has been reached. They think that with a good career and a high-paying salary, they have reached the top. But this is where the deep hunger begins.

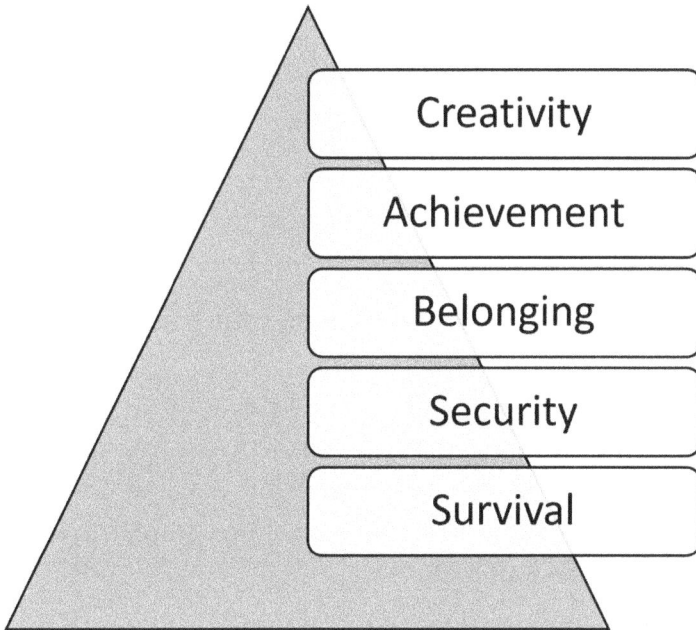

Figure 8   Human Needs

When all the other needs have been fulfilled, one remaining need is to **create something that will live beyond ourselves,** beyond our purpose for being here. When there are no other needs, we still must appreciate life itself and contribute to life in a way that will leave a memory of ourselves after we die. Some people depend on their offspring to fulfill this need. Others write books, invent, or teach.

A successful life is a created life.

Some people go through life without realizing they can have more. But a successful life is a created life. It doesn't just happen. You must look at yourself in the mirror. Get some clarity about where you are and what you are starting with. Understand your value. Know you are strong and that opportunities do exist.

🌱 KEY POINT

A successful life consists of the five human needs being met:

- Survival
- Security
- Belonging
- Achievement
- Creativity

Each of us has the capacity to create a successful life.

👣 ACTION STEPS

Use the pyramid of human needs and describe in your journal, which of the levels are being fulfilled in your life and how they are being fulfilled. If there are levels that are not yet being fulfilled, how would you like them to be fulfilled?

The Personal SWOT Analysis

SWOT stands for Strengths, Weaknesses, Opportunities, and Threats.

Strengths are what you do well. Your strengths can also be your relationships, especially with those who care about you and want to see you succeed. These people are your *Circle of Influence.*

Examples of strengths:

- I love to garden. One of my strengths is *growing vegetables.*

- I have a close group of friends that I keep in touch with on a regular basis. One of my strengths is *cherishing close friends.*

- I love to learn. One of my strengths is that *I learn what I need to learn in order to succeed in my business.*

A **weakness** is something about you that will not give you an edge; rather, it is something that could pull you down when you are trying to accomplish something. If there is something that you are not particularly good at doing, then you will probably not love doing it. Similarly, if you do not like doing something, but you need to do it anyway, then you might not be good at completing it. If someone in your life is negative toward you or does not support you or care about your success, then they are a weakness for you. These people would best be removed from your life or, if that isn't possible, then at least limit the effect you let them have in your life.

Examples of weaknesses:

- I have a sweet tooth. One of my weaknesses is *not always eating well.*

- I am not organized. One of my weaknesses is that *I don't keep track of my paperwork.*

- I have a chronic illness. One of my weaknesses is that *I lose my energy easily.*

Opportunities are things you could work with to improve your situation, things that could be utilized for your advantage. Usually, opportunities come and go and must be taken advantage of when they exist and before they fade away. They could be a person whom you could benefit from interacting with or an event that you could benefit from attending.

Examples of opportunities:

- Meeting someone at work who lives in your neighborhood and *wants to carpool*

- Reading a book on efficiency that includes *great suggestions*

- Finding a job that *pays 20 percent more and is ten miles closer to your home*

- Knowing a person who *specializes in work that is one of your weaknesses*

- Finding a location that *could potentially benefit your business*

- Registering for a conference that will *provide training you need*

Threats are things that come up that could work against you to hurt your situation. Threats could be long term and last for several days, months, or years, or they could exist only momentarily. They could be a person who might harm you if you interacted with them or an event that might be harmful. It is a good idea to know and understand the threats that exist so that you can minimize them and or avoid them altogether.

Examples of threats:

- Your child's school closes, and commuting to the new school *adds an hour to your day.*

- Your spouse decides to take their dream job, *over 500 miles away.*

- The doctor tells you that your *lab results are worrisome*, and you need more testing.

- You *depend on a single person* for key roles, and you do not understand the process they use.

- You *depend on only a single company*—a single source—to provide a key product.

- Your positive *cash flow depends on a single product or service.*

🌱 KEY POINT

By knowing your strengths and weaknesses, you will be aware of opportunities you can benefit from and threats that you can avoid.

👣 ACTION STEPS

List at least three strengths and possible opportunities that you would be attracted to for each. Then, list at least three weaknesses and possible threats that you would try to avoid because of them.

Archetype and Enneagram SWOT

The Enneagram types and archetypes each have strengths and weaknesses associated with them. If you have identified with a specific archetype and Enneagram, it might be helpful for you to understand the strengths and weaknesses associated with those personalities. In the event that certain opportunities or threats arise, at the very least, you will have an awareness of what those tendencies could be.

Enneagram	Strengths	Weaknesses
The Reformer	Passionate about making things better	Focused on perfection
The Helper	Loves to make a difference in the lives of others	Tends to put the needs of others before their own
The Achiever	Driven to be the best at whatever they do	Gets caught up in being successful and forgets who they are
The Individualist	Turns the ordinary into extraordinary	Tends to get stuck in their emotions and not stay in the present moment
The Investigator	Gets immense pleasure in observing and learning	Doesn't share what they have learned because they feel it's not complete
The Loyalist	Courageous, nothing can stand in their way	Becomes so focused on the goal that they disconnect from their purpose

The Enthusiast	Loves to live life to the fullest, open to all life has to offer	Hides from painful feelings which only makes them more painful
The Challenger	Intuitively knows what needs to be done and they make it happen	Others can feel intimidated by their seemingly aggressive behavior
The Peacemaker	Understands what it feels like to be in others' shoes	Hard time deciding because they don't like upsetting others

Table 7   Strengths and Weaknesses (Enneagrams)

Archetype	Strengths	Weaknesses
The Innocent	Optimistic, trusting, hopeful	In denial, naive, needs to feel safe
The Orphan	Independent, realistic, resilient	Complaining, tends to feel like the victim
The Hero	Determined, disciplined	Arrogant, ruthless, afraid of impotence
The Caregiver	Compassionate, generous, nurturing	Codependent, martyr-like, enabling

The Seeker	Autonomous, ambitious	Alienated, isolated, self-centered
The Rebel	Humble, capacity to change	Self-destructive, angry
The Lover	Passionate, enthusiastic, committed	Objectifies others, uses sexuality
The Creator	Creative, imaginative, visionary	Self-indulgent, obsessive, spoiled
The Jester	Free, lives in the moment	Irresponsible, inconsistent, slow
The Sage	Wise, knowledgeable, nonattached	Pompous, critical, judgmental
The Magician	Powerful, transformative	Manipulative, disconnected
The Ruler	Responsible, protective, managerial	Rigid, controlling, entitled

Table 8 Strengths and Weaknesses (Archetypes)

🌱 KEY POINT

Each Enneagram and archetype has inherent strengths and weaknesses associated with it.

👣 ACTION STEPS

Using the Enneagram and archetype you identified with earlier in the book, take a moment to write down the strength and weakness for each. Think about an experience in which you have utilized your strengths to benefit from an opportunity. Write down your thoughts. Now, think about an experience when a situation did not go well due to these weaknesses. Write down your thoughts.

Creating a Successful Life

The easiest way to make a positive change in your life is to use your SWOT. Look at what is happening around you and think about how your strengths can be combined with current opportunities. When you do, you might find that you get a bit excited at the thought of one of those combinations. If that something aligns with your purpose, you will feel it, and you will know it deep down. Sometimes it helps if you can imagine creating a business or beginning a career that uses a combination of a strength and an opportunity. For example, if you love to bake cookies and there is a coffee shop in town, you could offer to bake cookies and sell them at the coffee shop and give a percentage of the profits to the owner of the shop.

After you create your SWOT and come up with some ideas for a potentially viable business or career, the next step is to get clear on what people want. If your dream is owning a business, then the people you are thinking of are your future customers. If your dream is a new career, then the people you are thinking of are your future managers.

What could you do that combines your strengths with a current opportunity that would provide something that these people want or need?

1. Speed and convenience – they want an outcome fast, easy, and now.

2. Done for them – they want it done for them and then automated.

3. An awesome experience – they want to feel special.

4. Part of a leading edge – they want to get it before everyone else.

5. Human interaction – they want access to you.

In the example of baking cookies for the local coffee shop, the owner of the shop would like additional income. But customers coming into the shop might want the convenience of buying cookies (#1) while they purchase their coffee. The cookies are also already baked and ready to go so the customer would enjoy a "done for you" experience (#2). And, if the cookies are packaged creatively with individual handwritten inspirational notes, then the customer will feel special (#3) and they will also feel connected to you and to the coffee shop (#5).

Not every description will hit on more than one of these points, but if you have a business idea and you know what people want, then you could come up with an idea that will give people value and provide you with money.

And more importantly, a business like this will begin to satisfy the higher levels of your human needs, as discussed earlier. Specifically, the business will create income, which will provide more security to your life. You will be interacting with people at the coffee shop as well as the people who support your business (marketing, finance, and so on), and therefore, you will belong to a group of entrepreneurs. And being the owner of this business will give you an enormous sense of achievement. And finally, it will be something that you created—something that didn't exist before you created it.

The way to make something big happen is to see it first. Create the vision, see it, give it as much detail as possible, and then hold that vision in your mind. Even when your logical mind tries to tell you all the reasons why it could never happen, hold that vision in your mind. Think about all the reasons it is important to you, imagine it has already happened, see it in detail, and feel the emotions. And then, with all that held within you, create the plan in detail.

A good plan begins with the current situation but sees the destination. It chooses steps along the way, and it searches for opportunities to apply strengths in order to achieve those steps.

A *career plan* describes how you will go about reaching a certain position, what your career will be, and the steps to get there, step by step. A *business plan* describes how you will create your business, the steps to make it grow, the value provided, and the market that it will serve.

🌱 KEY POINT

You can create a successful life by connecting one of your strengths to an existing opportunity. Sometimes, you can even create a new opportunity!

👣 ACTION STEPS

Choose one of your strengths, preferably the one you like the most about yourself. Then close your eyes and visualize how you can connect that strength to the outside world. Whom will you serve, and what do they want? How will you create value for them?

What It Means to Connect

Innovation is the ability to associate random ideas, form a mental picture, and connect them in a way they have never been connected before to solve a problem or improve a situation. Receiving guidance is only the first part of the solution; making connections is important when taking steps forward after receiving guidance. The ability to remain present in the moment and have the vision to see the elements you have to work with at the time you are seeing them is critical too. But, neither of these things will give you the solution to take a step forward if you cannot connect them.

Deficient	Balanced	Excessive
Inconsistent	Articulate	Self-righteous
Unable to express thoughts	Artistic	Talkative
Unreliable	Centered	Arrogant
Manipulative	Present	Opinionated

Table 9 Your Ability to See Possibilities

The Thyroid Gland – The Physical Body's Truth

The thyroid gland is located at the base of your neck, in the front and just below your Adam's apple. It is associated with the **Throat Chakra**, which enables you to speak from your truth while remaining centered and in the moment. When I speak to others, whether it is to one or one hundred people, I make sure that I am receiving guidance from Source, blocking any negative thoughts that could detract from my message. Then I visualize God speaking through me. And He does speak through me. I just let myself relax into His loving arms, and the words just flow out of my mouth. The message that comes through me is always exactly what needs to be said, and I connect.

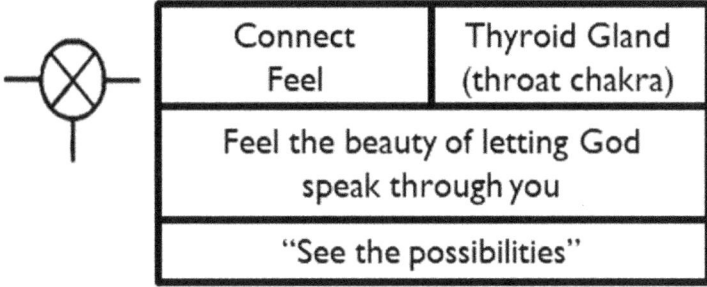

Connect Feel	Thyroid Gland (throat chakra)
Feel the beauty of letting God speak through you	
"See the possibilities"	

Figure 9   Connect and Feel

The thyroid gland produces hormones that control the body's metabolism, heart rate, digestion, muscle control, mood, and bone growth. It needs iodine to function properly, but too much iodine can be just as bad as not enough. Table salt has iodine added to it, but if you are on a sodium-restricted diet, you might be lacking in iodine.

Dairy products, especially Greek yogurt, are a good source of iodine, as is fish and shellfish.

The thyroid also needs selenium and zinc. Brazil nuts are a great source of selenium. Eggs are high in both zinc and iodine. Zinc can also be found in chicken and beef.

It is also a good idea to eat foods high in antioxidants like brightly colored berries. Stay away from foods that are highly processed.

The Mind – Mantras to Tune Your Mind to Connect and Feel
By opening your mind to the possibility of connecting the moment to your guidance, it shall be so. By letting Source guidance lead the way,

the throat chakra helps you to make the connections in exactly the way that is meant to be made.

Speak these words and allow yourself to make the connections needed to take the steps forward in the moment:

> *I am a creative and joyful messenger of light.*
> *As I speak, so shall it be.*

The **Throat Chakra** is the energy center located around the thyroid gland. It resonates with a light blue color. If it becomes off-balance, then you will begin to feel either deficient or excessive, and you will feel this imbalance in your ability to express your thoughts clearly in your spoken words.

You can tune your throat chakra in many ways:

Color: The resonant color of the throat chakra is a light blue. Focus on this color. Find something with this color, and carry it with you to remind you to focus.

Vibration: The resonant frequency of the throat chakra is solfeggio 741 Hz, which is natural G, or *Sol*. Listen to a solfeggio 741 Hz pure tone vibration (search Google for "741 tone throat chakra").

Sound: Listen to running water or falling rain or the piano.

Crystals: Turquoise, blue topaz, and azurite. Place the crystal on your throat as you meditate.

Herbs/Essential Oils: Geranium, chamomile, peppermint, cypress. Use the oil in a diffuser or rub a drop or two on your hand and smell the fragrance to remind you of your throat chakra.

Exercise: Gargle with warm water, vibrating the liquid in the back of your throat to stimulate the throat chakra.

Meditation/Prayer: Archangel Zadkiel, *the Righteousness of God.* Ask him to help you stay connected to your truth, to connect the present moment to your spiritual guidance, and to help you see the opportunities that are revealed by connecting your guidance to the moment.

🌱 KEY POINT

When your thyroid gland is healthy and resonating according to a healthy throat chakra energy center, it acts as a spiritual connector, allowing you to connect where you are to where you want to be and to visualize a better future.

👣 ACTION STEPS

The best way to improve the vibration and health of your thyroid gland is to open your mind to possibilities and let those thoughts flow through you. Choose one of your strengths and three people you know. In what way could each of these people benefit from your strength? Are there local events that might benefit from something you offer? Combine your strengths with people you know and local events to begin to see possibilities.

Ask Archangel Zadkiel to help keep you connected to your true self and to reveal the opportunities that are meant for you in your life journey.

Resonate

My Personal Navigation

When I was a child, my mother, the matriarch, shunned me. I was the black sheep. For the others to remain in good graces with my mother, they had to shun me too. So, I always felt like an outsider, like I didn't belong, that nobody really liked me and if they were acting like they did that it was either because they felt they had to or there was something they were trying to achieve in the family status.

I couldn't feel love, at least for other people. But I loved my animals.

Everything had gotten numbed inside of me so badly that I couldn't feel anything. I saw glimpses of what love looked like when I went to visit my friend Susie. In her home, the air felt alive, sparkly, and full of glitter. Her family's voices felt like music, soft and sweet. They hugged and said the words "I love you" to one another. It was like being on another planet.

But that was the life I wanted.

I thought I found it once when I was just nineteen. I married him at twenty-one. Looking back on this time in my life, it is obvious that I was too badly damaged to be able to love anyone. I didn't even love myself. I turned into a fawn so easily, just doing what I was told to do, even if it meant doing things that I wouldn't normally do. I was broken; he was broken too. I stayed for over ten years.

Taking time for myself after I left this relationship was critical in my healing. The counseling that I received taught me to pay attention to the things people did rather than the things they said or the way I wanted things to be. I learned to think rationally about how a person's behavior was indicative of the way they felt. Through this thinking, I came out of the fog and began trusting that others could love me.

When I met my husband Gary, I was much better at trusting that I could be loved. But I still didn't feel love. I only knew it was possible—and perhaps that is the beginning—but I didn't yet love myself, within myself. I kept a protective layer between my heart and the world, never quite opening up completely, even to my husband. Even though I wanted the best from others, and even though some of them never gave me reason to expect them to hurt me, I still expected the worst. Somewhere deep inside of me, I waited for them to hurt me.

The experience with Archangel Gabriel showed me a peek behind the curtain of what love could feel like. I was living as Gabriel. He was in me, with me; my feelings were his feelings. Although my body was still damaged, my airways were still hypersensitive, and I was still reacting to environmental dangers, my mind and my soul were merged with Gabriel for that year. I was able to think differently. I got to experience the feeling of complete safety and self-love. Those experiences began to create new memories and shift the beliefs from impossible to possible.

I began expressing love and trust and openness in my life that year. People would come to me as if they were being drawn to me. They were actually being drawn to Gabriel, but the experience for me was as if they were being drawn to me. I wanted to live my life like that forever, and it was because he embodied that love. It wasn't a guarded love. He was vibrating pure love.

We Attract What We Resonate

Although it took many years to finally awaken and become the person I was meant to be, I am not bitter about the journey. Like a piece of coal under pressure, the difficult things that happen in life might seem to be happening *to* you, but without them, you would not become the beautifully imperfect diamond you are meant to become. People look at me strangely when I tell them that I feel blessed to have gone through all I have gone through, that the experiences throughout my life have shaped me into the person I am today.

As I began healing and connecting to myself, and then speaking from that place inside that I had hidden from myself for my entire life, a certain kind of person noticed me. I barely had to make a noise. It was as if my thoughts alone were sending a song into the ether, and those who understood the beauty of my melody would hear and turn to notice where the music was coming from. They would look at me as if to say, *you understand!* And I did.

My journey had tuned my energetic body to vibrate and attract the people who were meant to be attracted to me. But first, I had to connect within myself and accept who I was, what I had gone through, and how it not only hadn't destroyed me, but it had made me who I am. All of this was according to the universal plan. Then, when I relaxed and let the energy of that flow through me, I realized my energetic body was sending out a song of hope.

Everything vibrates and sends rippling energy into the universe. You have no choice but to resonate. And all vibration is a form of music. You cannot stop the music, but you can choose the song. Marketing is not about selling; it is about connecting. It is about sharing yourself with others.

When you share your story about why you are doing what you are doing, the right people will be attracted to you and to your story. Just like bees are attracted to the flowers that vibrate at a specific frequency, you are vibrating at your own specific frequency, and you will attract the right people.

The music was there, emanating from within me, and when I finally got up the courage to be authentic and share one of my big scary truths about who I am and what I had been through, I put words to the music. I began to share the story about what I had been through. I shared that my "successful career" had felt like constant panic, but I had pushed myself so hard because I was so afraid that everything would fall apart. I shared that when everything finally did fall apart, and my heart stopped beating, I experienced the greatest blessing of my life—God's grace to finally be myself.

Who resonates with what you do?

Who needs what you provide?

Who Feels Your Energy?

Namaste means "the Light within me recognizes and loves the Light within you."

A tuning fork designed to vibrate at a certain frequency will vibrate without being touched when you play a note at that frequency and hold the tuning fork nearby.

Slow-motion photography shows that flowers vibrate at a specific frequency, and if we synthesize that frequency in nature, we will attract bees.

So, identify who you wish to impact and what they desire, and then focus your messaging to resonate with what they desire. Once you have their attention, give them what you know they need to obtain, what they desire.

Desire	Need
To meet the right man	To feel sexier and more confident

To live life on their own terms	To make more money
To travel	To have a passive income business
To lose weight	To feel loved and healthy

Table 10 Desires Versus Needs

🌱 KEY POINT

All vibration is a form of music. You attract what you resonate.

👣 ACTION STEPS

Think about how you are feeling right now, and in your journal, write down your answers to the following questions: How do you normally show up in life? Are you typically impatient? Are you generous? How would you like to show up? What kind of people would you like to attract into your life?

Resonate by Telling Your Story

Most epic stories use the device of "A Hero's Journey," which involves the main character setting off on a journey of crisis, struggling with a personal battle, and then returning victorious and transformed. For example, Dorothy in *The Wizard of Oz* goes on a long journey and returns with the realization that "there's no place like home." I believe we all have a hero's journey.

There are five main parts to a hero's journey:

1. **Before** – Before today, things were much different. Perhaps you were in a dull job, in an unhappy marriage, or in some other place that was not where you wanted to be.

2. **The Fall** – Even though you were in a place that was not perfect, you really had no big intention of changing things, until something totally surprising knocked you down to the bottom. If you had been in a dull job, you may have gotten fired. If you were in an unhappy marriage, you may have asked for a divorce.

3. **The Bottom** – Here at the bottom, life got very difficult, and you may not have known how you were ever going to survive. You may have been really depressed, maybe living on the street and not knowing where your next meal was going to come from.

4. **The Struggle** – You struggled to make your life better. It was not easy. It seemed that every time you thought you would take a step forward, something would happen to knock you backward.

5. **After** – And now your life is pretty good. You are happy. Maybe you own your own business now, are happily married. Where you are now is better than where you were before. And because of the experience, you have realized something important about yourself, and it is related to your life purpose.

🌱 KEY POINT

We all have been knocked down. We all have struggled to get back up. It is up to us to learn from the experience and learn about ourselves in the process.

👣 ACTION STEPS

What is your hero's journey?

What It Means to Resonate

When something *resonates* with you, it causes you to feel an attraction to it; you begin to understand and feel in common with whatever you are attracted to. When someone else is attracted to you and your message, it is because you are resonating in a way that is causing them to be attracted to you.

The ability to resonate is the ability to emit authentic emotions. The keyword is *authentic*. When you give yourself permission to feel deeply about something and then speak from those same emotions, you automatically attract others who are also feeling those same emotions. Even if they have not articulated those feelings yet, if you speak authentically, then you will resonate and attract those who feel in common with you.

In order to resonate at your highest vibration, you need to feel emotionally stable, balanced, and secure with who you are. That does not mean you need to have full clarity about your vision or your purpose—in fact, speaking about your feelings regarding *not* having clarity is itself authentic and will create resonance with others who are also having insecurities about this. It is more important to share what is coming up for you than it is to have your message clear.

When you are tense or critical and demand that people listen to what you say, you resonate so strongly that you push people away. If you are indecisive and afraid to let go and be real, you will not resonate strongly enough, and people will not be attracted to what you are saying. To enable people to resonate with you and want to hear more of what you are saying, your communications must originate from that place of unconditional love—from your true self within and from your heart.

Deficient	Balanced	Excessive
Paranoid	Feeling loved unconditionally	Very critical
Indecisive	Emotionally balanced	Moody
Feeling unloved	Empathic	Possessive
Feeling sorry for yourself	Compassionate	Demanding

Table 11   Your Ability to Resonate Love

The thymus gland is located just below the sternum, the hard bone in the center of your upper chest. The sternum protects both your heart and your thymus gland, which is critical to the production of T cells for your immune system. This is also where your **Heart Chakra** is located. By tapping on your sternum, you stimulate both your thymus gland and your heart chakra. Stimulating your thymus gland helps improve your immune system, and stimulating your heart chakra helps you to feel more connected to gratitude. It is the feeling of gratitude that centers you in your true and authentic self.

You can maintain the health of your thymus gland in these important ways:

- Take antioxidants: vitamins C and E.

- Exercise daily, especially cardio and stretching, to increase blood flow.

- Practice gratitude, compassion, letting go, and staying clear of judgment.

- Tap the sternum to stimulate the thymus gland.

- Eat fresh vegetables, especially cruciferous ones, such as cauliflower, broccoli, cabbage

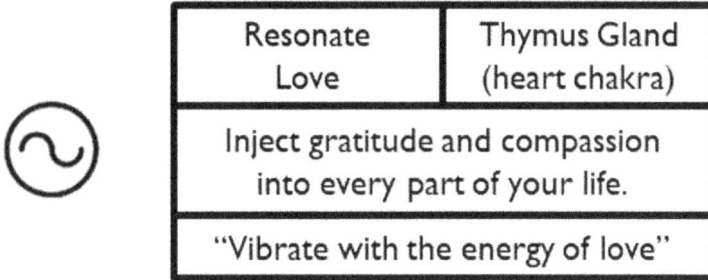

Resonate Love	Thymus Gland (heart chakra)
Inject gratitude and compassion into every part of your life.	
"Vibrate with the energy of love"	

Figure 10 Resonate Love

By opening your mind to the possibility that there is something in each moment to be grateful for, you are creating a resonance of gratitude. There always is something to be grateful for.

Sit in a firm chair with your feet flat on the floor, or lie down on a firm but soft surface. Place both hands, left over right, on top of your heart. Close your eyes and begin relaxing your head, your shoulders, and your neck. Sit up straight so that your lungs can expand, and then begin breathing more deeply but at a relaxed pace. Begin tapping gently with your right hand and focus on the vibration that it causes. Then, with your eyes still closed and continuing to tap gently, think of something or someone in your life that, if they were to be gone tomorrow, would make you sad. Even if it is something as simple as the bed that you sleep in each night. Focus on the gratitude that you feel in this moment.

Then, speak these words to tune your mind to feel gratitude deeply and resonate the frequency of love into all that you are:

I am at peace with myself and with others.
I am grateful for my health, my abundance, and my friends.
As I speak, so shall it be.

The **Heart Chakra** is the energetic body's song. It is the energy center located above the thymus gland. It resonates with either the color green or the color pink. If it resonates with the color green, it is focused on healing. If it resonates with the color pink, it is focused on love. In this section, we are focusing only on the heart chakra resonating with love and compassion, and therefore, to the color pink.

If heart chakra energy becomes imbalanced, you may feel either deficient or excessive, and you feel this imbalance in your ability to feel grateful. Instead, you begin to worry, feel resentment toward others, and perhaps feel sorry for yourself.

You can tune your heart chakra in many ways:

Color: The resonant color of the heart chakra is pink. Focus on this color. Find something with this color, and carry it with you to remind you to focus on love, compassion, and gratitude.

Vibration: The resonant frequency of the heart chakra is solfeggio 639 Hz, which is natural F or *Fa*. Listen to a solfeggio 639 Hz pure tone vibration (search Google for "639 tone heart chakra").

Sound: Listen to music from the pipe organs.

Crystals: Jade, rose quartz, green tourmaline, kunzite. Place the crystal over your heart as you meditate.

Herbs/Essential Oils: Eucalyptus, spearmint, rose bulgar. Use the oil in a diffuser or rub a drop or two on your hand and smell the fragrance to remind you of your heart chakra.

Exercise: Use two hands to make the sign of a heart; visualize it connected to a bright white light.

Meditation/Prayer: Archangel Chamuel, *the Sight of God*. Ask Chamuel to help you stay connected to gratitude, to inject compassion into every part of your life, to enable you to feel the love of God, and to see the humanity of others through eyes of forgiveness.

KEY POINT

When our thymus gland is healthy and resonating according to a healthy heart chakra energy center, it acts as a spiritual oscillator, creating a strong vibration of love energy and sending that resonance out into the world around us.

ACTION STEPS

To improve the vibration and health of your thymus gland, focus on gratitude by reading the book *Attitudes of Gratitude* by M. J. Ryan. Read only one chapter per day, and then spend the day reflecting on what you have learned. At night before going to bed, write your thoughts in your journal.

Find a nice jar or wide-mouth vase to use as your gratitude jar. Buy colorful notepaper about 3" x 3" square. Each morning, write three things you are grateful for using three separate slips of paper. Fold them and put them into the jar. If someday you find yourself without anything to feel grateful for, reach into your gratitude jar, and read one of those notes.

Focus

My Personal Navigation

Before my NDE, I was an intense person. I would sit and work on something until it was done like a pit-bull. But it was an addiction; I was searching to fill an empty place inside of me. I thought achievement would do that. It never gave me the excitement that you get down "there," in that place in your pelvic floor when something really excites you passionately. It was ego-based and I would think: How this is going to look if I do this well? It was all externally driven.

After my NDE, everything was very spastic in my body, including my pelvic floor. The vagus nerve runs through all the organs and also innervates the muscles of the pelvic floor through the sacral vertebrae S2, S3, and S4. When you feel deeply passionate and excited about something (including, but not only, sexually), this area feels tingly and alive.

Since my autonomic nervous system was not functioning correctly, my pelvic floor became hypertonic along with my vocal cords and the sphincter that separates my stomach from the lower part of my esophagus (LES). I am sure that there were many other areas within my body that were experiencing the spasms, but these two were causing the most immediate problems.

Because my right vocal cord was experiencing semi-paralysis, my vocal tone was incredibly flat. Talking for any amount of time was exhausting. There were days when I couldn't talk for more than five minutes at a time before I needed a break.

I couldn't focus. I would try to sit and work on something the way I had done before, but my physical body was not used to focusing on something simply for the passion of purpose. It had always focused intensely for the badge of achievement.

I kept receiving flashes of inspiration surrounding the method that this book describes but I couldn't focus on it in a way that felt clear enough to express it to the world around me. The ideas would sweep into my mind. My body would react to the excitement, and the ideas would disappear into a black hole.

I had to learn to control the excitement, to breathe into it.

Authentic Power

Before I had my NDE and crossed over, I had no trouble focusing. In fact, it was just the opposite. When I set my sights on a goal, I would focus on it so intensely, I sometimes wouldn't sleep. I would create an absurdly unrealistic goal, and then I would throw myself so hard into achieving that goal that everything else in my life was pushed to the side.

I was intensely focused, but not on the right things and certainly not for the right reasons. Being busy was a badge of honor, a flag I could wave in the air and show people I was achieving my goals in life. I was keeping busy because deep down inside, I feared that if I wasn't busy, I didn't matter.

When I went to bed at night, my mind would race over all the things that I had to do the next day. And when I woke up the next morning, my mind would begin by immediately racing over those same things all over again. I would always plan to do ten times the number of things I could ever have accomplished, and my feet would be running before they even hit the floor. By the end of the day, I would be so exhausted that I would collapse into bed, but my mind was still racing, so it was usually hard for me to fall asleep.

When I started getting sick, I began to panic because I didn't have the energy to do all the things I needed to do (or thought I needed to do). One day, I began to cry to my husband about everything building up inside of me, terrified about the things I thought I needed to do, and acting like the world would end if I didn't get everything done.

He said these few words that stopped me in my tracks: "You don't *have* to do anything."

To this day, I think about those words and give thanks for how my life has changed. I am no longer being chased by my fears. I see others who are still trapped in that paradigm, and my heart feels deeply for them. And it's not as simple as deciding the dishes can sit in the sink overnight. It's about juggling chainsaws. It is feeling the need to say "yes" to taking on one more chainsaw, and one more after that, tap dancing while you are juggling and not realizing that you can really just step back and let everything drop to the floor. The world will not come to an end if you just let everything fall.

It's okay. Your soul really didn't want to be juggling chainsaws anyway!

And besides, there is something else you were meant to be focusing on.

🌱 KEY POINT

It is impossible to focus on your purpose and authentic power when you are controlled by fear.

👣 ACTION STEPS

Does your mind race with a million things that you feel you must get done?

Open your journal and list all the things that are worrying you and all the things that you feel you must do. After you feel you have captured the entire list, write down how your *physical* body is feeling. Is your heart racing? Is your stomach clenched? This is how your body feels when you are full of fear.

Now, write down a solution statement for each of these things that would alleviate and resolve the stress. For example, if one of the things is that you constantly worry about finances, you might write *"with an additional $1,200 per month income, I would not be worried about finances."* Write a solution for each of your worries.

Read on to learn how to move toward the solutions.

Create a Simple Plan

When I decided I was going to simplify my life, I first created an elaborate plan full of strategic milestones and elaborate goals that linked to each other. I attached the dates I would accomplish each one, bought a planner, and loaded up my calendar with things to do to ensure I would meet my goals.

When I was finished, I sat back, exhausted, feeling like I would puke. My heart was racing, my throat was tight, and fear gripped me so tightly I didn't do anything that first day. The next day, I decided it was okay that I took the day off because I had spent so much energy planning my new life. The following day, I found everything and anything else to focus on except what was in my plan.

A week later, I realized my problem was that I needed to learn more about this new life I wanted, and if I learned more about this new life, then I would feel more comfortable moving forward. So, I bought more courses, went to more seminars, downloaded more checklists. I joined Facebook groups and read books. But inside, I was still frozen; I knew what I needed to do, but it felt so foreign. Throughout my corporate career, I had set goals for myself and exceeded them. I had helped other people set goals for themselves. I had mentored younger engineers and managed senior scientists successfully. Why was this so hard?

I tried spending more money. I tried hiring personal coaches.

But, the more I tried to focus on my goals intellectually, the more my inner self put her fingers in her ears, shut her eyes tight, and chanted: *Na-nah, nah-nah, nah!* Finally, I realized that I was trying to do things the way I had always done things, and Inner Self was having none of that.

So, I put that planner on the shelf. I leaned back and focused my imagination on the life I wanted, the life that my inner self wanted.

I knew what I wanted, including:

- No debt and enough money so I would never have to worry about finances ever again

- To do things with my time that would give my life meaning

- Never work for a corporation ever again. In fact, I didn't even want to work for anyone else, just me.

- A *simple* life—to eat healthy, to have a flexible schedule, to sleep in if I wanted to, and to share my knowledge with others

I visualized our home, on many acres with a pond and a garden; there were goats and chickens, and I was canning fruits and vegetables. I saw small groups coming to my home, and I was sharing knowledge with them. I was at bookstores, signing my books. I didn't want a big house on the beach. I didn't want fancy cars or clothes or jewelry. I just wanted the chaos to stop. I just wanted enough money so that I could spend my time giving my life more meaning.

I wanted to spend my time giving my life more meaning.

Then, with a vision of my future set within my mind's eye, I created a new plan. A simple plan.

After the life that I had just released, the little girl inside of me was cringing at the idea of following a plan. I knew if I were to get to the future I wanted, I would have to keep things simple and focus. So, I used my vision as my goal. In my vision, I was living on a farm, gardening and canning and tending to a small flock of chickens and a few goats. I had finished my book, and I was attending book signings and speaking to small groups.

A good goal is bound by three things:

1. The date that the goal must be reached (schedule)

2. The maximum amount of money that can be spent to reach the goal (cost)

3. A clear definition of what the goal looks like when it is completed (quality)

Following this structure, my goal looked like this:

Within three years (schedule), for less than $25,000 (cost), I will become financially free; working for myself; doing things that give my life meaning; with a flexible work schedule; simple life; and a peaceful, healthy, and happy home (quality).

Then I created some milestones, which are also bound by schedule, cost, and quality:

Milestone #1 – Get out of debt via Dave Ramsey course/coaching within one year for $500 max

Milestone #2 – Sell home and buy farm within two years/$0.00 swap costs; use equity toward debt

Milestone #3 – Develop method, course, seminars, and products within two years for $5,000 or less

Milestone #4 – Write and self-publish my book within three years for $5,000 or less

Up until the decision to finally change my life, I had been carrying the responsibility of handling the bills myself, so my husband wouldn't know how deeply in debt we were. I had tried to climb out of the pit on my own so many times before, creating spreadsheets and getting consolidation loans. But I always ended up back where I started, or worse.

This time, I got serious and paid for some coaching. The hardest part was getting my husband on board. It's hard enough to make big changes yourself, but we both had to make big changes in our lives, starting with our mindset. Dave Ramsey worked for us, and although it seemed hard at the time, looking back at the experience, the only real difficulty was making the decision. Once we decided, it was easy. The other milestones were the same: It was only hard to decide we were getting out of debt, period. Once we decided to sell our house and buy a farm, things moved quickly. Our house sold in one day and settled in three weeks. We negotiated, paid off our debt, and rented an apartment for a few months while we looked for the perfect farm. We knew what we wanted, focused on it, and visualized us already living there. Then, when we found it, we moved in within forty-five days.

If I had wanted these things to happen more quickly, I could have spent more money. If I had wanted a big following for my business right away, then I could have hired a marketing expert, a web developer, and assorted other professionals to do a bunch of work for me. I decided that I didn't want to push or stress. Instead, I wanted everything to come to us, according to God's plan, because I trusted in that plan and had faith. The parameters in the milestones above were good enough for me.

🌱 KEY POINT

By creating a simple and clear plan toward a goal, you can create a life in which you spend more time giving your life more meaning.

👣 ACTION STEPS

Visualize a day in the future when you are spending it exactly the way you would want to, once you have arrived at your perfect future. Then using my example above, write out your goal and no more than four milestones that can take you to that goal:

Goal: Within x years (schedule) and for less than $\$x$ (cost) I will be _____ (quality).

Milestone #1

Milestone #2

Milestone #3

Milestone #4

Use Metrics to Measure Your Progress

When you are in the middle of working toward your goal, it may be hard to see how you are progressing. Sometimes, it may feel like you aren't making any progress at all.

Developing *metrics*—measurements—to assess your milestones at the beginning of your journey is an easy way to get a feel for how well you are progressing toward your final goal. As you create your milestones, think about what you can assess (measure) quickly along the way to get an estimate of schedule, cost, and quality.

The purpose of a metric is to provide a way to easily see progress and to adjust as necessary.

A metric is a way of measuring something. Here are a few examples:

- Length is a metric for distance.
- Degrees are a metric for temperature.
- Price is a metric for value.

In a plan, milestone metrics are used to track the schedule, cost, and quality of the milestones. After you have created metrics for each milestone, review them at regular intervals to see how well things are moving toward your final goal. The plan can be adjusted if needed.

In my example, for milestone #1—get out of debt via Dave Ramsey course/coaching within one year for $500 max—a set of metrics could be:

- Time remaining in the one year allotted (schedule)
- Amount of money spent on coaching (cost)
- Amount of debt remaining (quality)

With these three metrics, I was easily able to see my progress with that milestone.

🌱 KEY POINT

Metrics help you see how far along you are and whether adjustments are needed.

👣 ACTION STEPS

For each of the milestones you created in the previous section, think of a way to measure how far along you are. For each milestone accounting for schedule, cost, and quality, there should also be a separate metric for each.

Cash Flow

I was raised to believe that using debt wisely was a good thing—a tool that could help you leverage your finances. Well, that never worked out well for me. I'm reminded of this quote:

> *The rich rule over the poor, and the borrower is slave to the lender.*
> — Proverbs 22:7 (NIV)

I think people don't do well with debt because it sucks money out of their cash flow without giving them a feeling of accomplishment.

I am sure you have heard the saying, *Cash flow is the lifeblood of your household*. That means in order to keep a roof over your head, food on the table, and clothes on your back, your cash flow must be positive. Your income must be greater than your expenses, whether you are working for a paycheck or owning your own business. The income you bring into your home must be greater than your household expenses.

When you use credit to make a purchase, you have the positive feeling from the purchase itself, but you don't have the negative feeling from parting with any cash. A month later, you part with the cash, and the balance of what you owe decreases, but not as much as you just paid. So, you have a little bit of a negative feeling but no positive feeling. The next month, the same thing happens. And the next month. And the next. Meanwhile, you are getting hungry for a positive feeling.

It is a trap! And each month, money is being sucked out of your cash flow for something that just gives you negative feelings.

Maybe you get another credit card and buy something else to try again to capture some of that good feeling. Maybe a new car. Maybe you go out to dinner or take a vacation and put it all on your credit card. As the bills start to roll in, your cash flow gets squeezed.

FACT: Without positive cash flow, it is just a matter of time before you are bankrupt.

*You must design your **life** and your **business** so that your cash flow will always be positive.*

$$CASH\ FLOW = (\$\ IN - \$\ OUT) / TIME$$

Figure 11   Cash Flow Equation

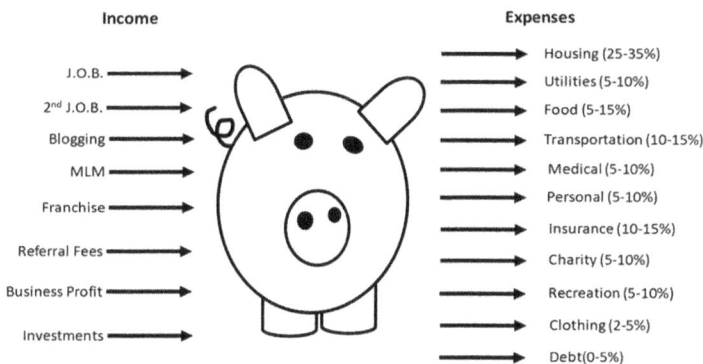

Figure 12   Feed the Pig

Here again is the Feed the Pig diagram (Figure 12). This is how I focused on the first milestone, "getting out of debt." I kept going over these numbers, finding ways to reduce the expenses and increase the income until the cash flow was positive. Each month, I would send the surplus of income directly to the debt that remained. Within a year, the debt was gone, and the surplus was still there. Since then, the surplus is going into savings.

🌱 KEY POINT

Cash flow is the simplest way to visualize and control your finances.

👣 ACTION STEPS

List your expenses. Are you within the percentages listed in the *Feed the Pig* diagram? What could you do to reduce your expenses? What could you do that would both increase your income and give your time more meaning?

What It Means to Focus on the Flow

Being focused and in the flow is being in a state of feeling fully immersed in enjoyment and fulfillment. When you are in this state, you lose your sense of space and time; your awareness is only of what you are focusing on, and time becomes meaningless. You will know you are in the flow when everything seems to disappear except what you are focused on, and your thought stream becomes clear. When you are in the flow, everything you are working on seems to make perfect sense and is incredibly easy.

The ability to focus deeply and slide into a state of flow depends on your **Sacral Chakra**, which is associated with your pelvic floor and your sexual organs. Your ability to feel passion applies to all areas of your life, including sexual passion, but also your passion for your purpose. If the vibration of your sacral chakra is low, then you may be feeling as though you are burying some emotions and come across to others as shy and untrusting. And if your sacral chakra is vibrating at too high a frequency, then you may have aggression issues and come across as manipulative. Either too high or too low, you may find that you have a hard time focusing. If you take steps to balance your sacral chakra, you may find that you begin to feel friendlier and more intuitive. As you relax into this balanced state, you will find that you have more and more moments where you feel deeply in a flow state.

Deficient	Balanced	Excessive
Resentful	Creative	Aggressive
Shy	Friendly	Emotionally volatile
Untrusting	Intuitive	Manipulative
Emotionally unavailable	Considerate	Self-serving

Table 12 Ability to Focus on Flow

The Pelvic Floor is a set of muscles that are supported by the pelvic and hypogastric nerves that originate from the sacral nerve roots. This mesh of nerves is part of the autonomic nervous system conveying information of either attraction or repulsion and helping you to focus on what you want.

Focus Flow	Gut Brain (sacral chakra)
Let go of a painful past. Let only joy and harmony flow through your life	
"Focus only on flow and ease"	

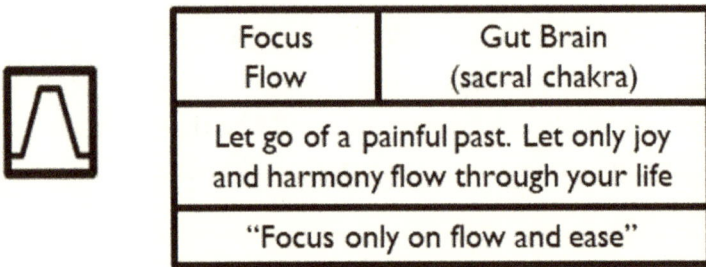

Figure 13 Focus on the Flow

My sacral chakra was a mess because of my painful childhood. I had become a workaholic in order to numb the emotions from my painful childhood. On the outside, I was really successful and looked like I had it all together, but inside I was screaming in panic at the chaos. People were amazed at my ability to develop strategies for successful programs and projects. I was really good at it because it was natural for me, but it wasn't healthy for me.

The **Sacral Chakra** is the energy center that is located below the navel and behind the bladder. It is that area you may associate with sexual excitement. If it becomes imbalanced, then you will begin to feel either deficient or excessive, and you will feel this imbalance in your ability to focus. Instead, you will begin to feel fearful and concerned that you may not be focusing on the right things.

By asking Source/God for guidance in healing your sacral chakra and gut-brain, you are opening your mind to the possibility of connecting to flow. There is something so simple and beautiful in asking. When you are alone, when nobody else is watching and you have only yourself to be embarrassed by, then ask for help. Lie down flat, no pillow. Put both hands on your stomach, palms down, just below your ribs. Inhale and feel your breathing move your stomach up and down. As you begin to relax, inhale deeply and into your belly so your belly pushes out as far as it will go. Hold there for a moment before forcibly blowing the air out—like you would blow out a candle—so completely that you can feel your diaphragm move up and your stomach become concave. Do this several times as you ask for healing of your sacral chakra. Ask that your sacral chakra be balanced and your gut-brain—or the *enteric nervous system*—be healthy. Ask for the ability to focus on your flow.

By asking Source/God for guidance in healing your sacral chakra, you are opening your mind to the possibility of allowing focus.

Then repeat these words to allow you to focus on your journey:

> *I have enough.*
> *I know enough.*
> *I am enough.*
> *My mind is clear, and I know the steps I am supposed to take.*
> *As I speak, so shall it be.*

Here are specific ways you can tune your sacral chakra:

Color: The resonant color of the sacral chakra is orange. Focus on this color. Find something with this color, and carry it with you to remind you to focus on your plan and your goal.

Vibration: The resonant frequency of the sacral chakra is solfeggio 417 Hz, which is natural D, *Re*. Listen to a solfeggio 417 Hz pure tone vibration (search Google for "417 tone sacral chakra").

Sound: Listen to trombone, tuba, and other low instruments.

Crystals: Pink tourmaline, coral, carnelian.

Herbs/Essential Oils: Mandarin red, patchouli, bergamot, clary sage. Use the oil in a diffuser or rub a drop or two on your hand, and smell the fragrance to remind you of your sacral chakra.

Exercise: Inhale deeply and push out your abdomen as far as you can. Hold it there and then exhale quickly while pulling your abdomen in and up. The pelvic floor should expand on the inhale and contract on the exhale. Repeat.

Meditation/Prayer: Archangel Jophiel, *Beauty of God*. Ask Jophiel to help you stay focused on your purpose, to give you the intuition needed to continue taking the steps forward according to your plan.

KEY POINT

When the muscles of your pelvic floor are healthy and toned without being hyper-tonic (spastic and stiff) and are resonating according to a healthy sacral chakra energy center, they will act as a spiritual band-pass filter, helping you to focus on your passion in a healthy way.

ACTION STEPS

To improve the vibration and health of your gut, focus on your intuition, and trust that what you feel is your personal truth is truly your truth. Pray to Archangel Jophiel to help you stay focused on the path.

Allow

My Personal Navigation

Before I got so sick, I was the perfect example of someone with excessive solar plexus energy: doing a lot but not always getting very much done, all the time worrying that I wasn't doing enough. I was a workaholic, and like any addiction, it was not good for my health. For someone who was always told as a child she didn't matter, having the career I had was like a drug. My career meant that I could accomplish big things, and being a person that accomplished big things meant that I did matter. So, I craved more responsibility because with the responsibility came accomplishment.

I thought there was nothing I couldn't do if I put my mind to it. My body had its limits, however.

The stress I had been putting on myself for years took its toll. I survived a third-degree heart block only because my husband had seen me turning blue and rushed me to the hospital. After the doctors got my heart beating, I arrested again, and they rushed me into surgery to implant a pacemaker. The doctors said I may have been having heart arrhythmias for days.

It was no surprise that I suffered a hypoxic traumatic brain injury as a result.

After the doctors installed a pacemaker and stabilized my heart, I slowly began to gain consciousness and interact with people. My body hurt, mostly my legs. It felt like they were on fire, especially my feet. I had no control over my bowels. I couldn't eat or drink without choking, and what I did get down, I usually couldn't keep down.

It felt like my entire nervous system was sunburned. My brain was jingling. Sounds were chaotic, loud and distorted. Lights were sharp and pierced through my eyes and into my brain. My skin felt prickly; the slightest touch felt magnified, and when I perspired, it felt like I was sweating battery acid.

Those who came to visit me must have felt that I had lost so much. But for me, the most incredible thing was that, energetically, I felt bigger than my physical body, much bigger. I felt pure joy at what I had experienced. I felt so much love. I started a journal, noting each nurse's name and what they did for me. The nurse's assistant who washed the vomit out of my hair. Even the cleaning man who listened to me when I asked that he not use anything with a strong smell to wash my floor. He was especially kind. My energy, my "presence" was larger than my hospital room. It was larger than the entire hospital building.

But I couldn't control my physical body. I would think about moving my foot and it would just shake. I could talk but I couldn't answer questions. The ideas would begin to form and then get sucked down a black hole. I couldn't follow a finger from side to side without my eye muscles going into a spasm.

I was faced with something I couldn't accomplish by pushing harder—getting well again.

I spent three weeks in the hospital before I was stable enough to be moved to a rehabilitation center. I spent two weeks there as an inpatient and then another six months as an outpatient. They taught me how to live with my new body. They taught me how I could communicate with my legs again. They explained the cranial nerves to me, taught me vestibular exercises to retrain my brain and calm down the dizziness, taught me how to swallow liquids without choking, and they gave me strategies for avoiding bright lights and loud noises.

They also helped me to understand that there is a difference between simply saying something and answering a question. These two functions are quite different. Answering a question requires much more brain processing.

As soon as I was able to walk with just a cane, I bought a card for each person in my journal from my hospital stay. I wrote a personal note inside of each card, describing what they had done for me when I needed them so much. I thanked them for their kindness and for helping me in my first steps toward recovery. I also bought a card for the hospital director. Inside, I put a letter explaining what each person had done for me and how much I appreciated them. I thanked her for the staff she had in place for me when I needed them. I had never done anything like this before. I could tell Gabriel was gone, and now it was up to me to keep all that he had taught me.

When I was able to walk up and down three steps in the rehab center, I was discharged. But my PT doctors told me that it was just the beginning of my journey back. They said I should continue the exercises that we had been doing and to remember that the tortoise wins the race.

I had always had a gym membership, and even though I got sick, I kept paying the $45-monthly membership fee because I was determined to get back there and get back on my feet. And there I was, walking with a cane, weak and off-balance, wearing earplugs and sunglasses to help mute the heightened sensory issues. There I was, going into that building, signing in as a member while leaning on my cane. There I was, climbing up on the treadmill, hooking my cane on the side of the machine, holding on tight and walking.

Even if it was ten minutes, even if it was once a week, I did it because I knew there were things I was meant to do, like developing my GPS method and writing this book. I knew that there were people who needed to hear my message. Although it was hard, by allowing my path to flow with grace, even with the pain, I gained the strength I needed to pick up a pen and begin writing.

Letting Yourself Allow

Before my near-death experience, I always had to be doing something, always panicking about something, always spinning the wheels of my mind. Looking back on it, I don't know what would have happened if I didn't have a million things on my mind and a long to-do list, but I never relaxed enough to find out. I was always pushing, always planning, always strategizing.

And, it was never good enough for me.

The closer I got to achieving a goal, the more I thought about the next goal afterward. I earned a bachelor's degree in electrical engineering at night while working full time during the day. But before the diploma was in my hands, I had already applied for moving on and getting my master's degree in electrical engineering. And less than two years after receiving that degree, I applied for another master's degree in industrial engineering.

I'm certain some people thought I was smart and driven, but the truth was I was running from my own thoughts. I was terrified. I never felt successful. It was a charade.

And once I realized I was supposed to create this method and teach people how to use it so that they can receive guidance and walk their life path according to that guidance, I began to realize what real success meant and how difficult it was for me to physically reach goals directly tied to who I really am. Creating the method, writing this book, being vulnerable with who I really am, and how I got to where I am was hard. This was real success, and the closer I got, the more my body felt like running and hiding.

People who have experienced trauma may associate the excitement of success with the same physiological reactions as trauma. They avoid subjecting themselves to excitement inducing circumstances, which causes them to be almost phobic about success.

– Susanne Babbel, PhD, MFT[7]

Self-sabotage was real for me. I would work hard to reach a goal, and the closer I got to that goal, the more I was filled with something I didn't recognize as fear. It was physiological. My body was reacting in a way that I couldn't understand. Something would swell up inside of me and take control. My heart rate, my blood pressure, even the way my lungs took in air felt shallow and heavy and labored. The more I pushed my willpower to assert control over the *thing* that was welling up inside of me, the more control it had.

I tried to ignore it, pretending everything was okay, pretending it was my imagination, pretending I was stronger than it, but sometimes nothing worked. At times, my efforts instead led to me becoming so paralyzed with fear that I felt nearly catatonic. I wouldn't be able to work on those days; I couldn't talk on the phone. The only thing I knew to do was to find a repetitive motion. I would stay there for hours, focusing on the repetition and blocking out my thoughts, so I could just sink into the detached depths of my mind where I knew it was safe. Sometimes the repetitive motion was rubbing my leg; sometimes it was picking at my skin. Sometimes I played a video game. Sometimes I simply twirled my hair. I would hear a plane fly overhead and the clock on the wall ticking, but I couldn't talk, I couldn't move—I wasn't there. It was what I knew from my childhood. It was safe.

Eventually, I would crawl out of my fugue state and return to my *normal life*, exhausted and empty. Sometimes the goal I had been working toward remained intact but seemed less intimidating. Other times it had passed, and I had missed out on the opportunity, which made me feel both relieved and worthless.

---

7 Babbel, Susanne. "Fear of Success." *Psychology Today.* January 3, 2011. psychologytoday.com/us/blog/somatic-psychology/201101/fear-success

If you try something and fail, you go back to what you knew. You may not be happy about it, but you go back to your comfort zone. If you try something and succeed, you head into uncharted territory. Things are different. Things change.

— James Sudakow[8]

Self-sabotage is not a weakness; it is a physiological response based on fear and the need to survive. It is abusive to fight our fear. It's not out to get us; it is here to protect us, to serve us. If we make fear the enemy instead of seeing it as a normal part of being human and taking risks, then we risk turning fear into an endless treadmill that exhausts us and ultimately fails.

Learning to flow *with* fear rather than letting it paralyze me was an essential, prerequisite skill for me in order to succeed at anything. The first step of learning to flow with fear was understanding how I looked at fear and the patterns that existed. Some people ignore their fears around needing to please others. Some people punish themselves if they self-sabotage. Some people pretend things are perfect if they have issues with perfectionism.

It is hard to think about how we look at fear. It is harder to change the way we think about fear. But we are all here for a purpose, and we must be brave.

Being brave does not mean to feel the fear and do it anyway. It does not mean to focus on your goal and let all else be damned.

Being brave is being wise. It means blocking out judgment from outside voices and, instead, tuning inward to your guidance, which sometimes tells you that it isn't the right time and to turn around. Sometimes turning around is the bravest thing you can do—if that is

8 Sudakow, James. "Why Fear of Success Is Holding You Back More Than Fear of Failure." *Inc.* July 26, 2019. inc.com/james-sudakow/why-fear-of-success-is-holding-you-back-more-than-.html

what the voice inside the deepest, quietest, stillest place in your heart is telling you to do.

Being brave is being true to yourself and trusting yourself more than you trust the crowd, even if it means letting them all think you are a coward.

My near-death experience changed the way I think about fear. It gave me the opportunity to stand outside of myself, outside of these three dimensions, beyond this time and this space, and see fear. It gave me the choice to change the way I think about fear. Today, almost four years after the event, my body still sometimes reacts as if it is terrified because, physically, it was programmed to react a certain way. But there are things that I want to accomplish in my lifetime, goals that I am meant to complete, and people that I am meant to impact. I knew that I must be brave.

KEY POINT

Being brave is being wise enough to recognize when your body is sensing fear and not letting it paralyze you, and then listening instead to your inner guidance.

ACTION STEPS

Do you remember a time when you wanted to achieve something, but you felt overwhelmed, and you shrank back instead of moving forward? How did that make you feel? Open your journal and write about how your life could be different today if you hadn't stopped yourself. Review your goal and milestones from the chapter on Focus and note how your body reacts.

Your Milestone Plan Is Your Map

The best way to accomplish something is to use a milestone plan. Earlier in the Focus chapter, you created a simple milestone plan as your map to stay focused on your vision, keep organized, and keep moving. As you reach each milestone, pause and reflect on how you achieved success. Praise yourself and let gratitude flow through you. Don't immediately jump to the next thing on your milestone plan. Instead, take a moment, an hour—even a day—to lean back into the arms of God and give thanks for the moment.

As you follow your plan, if something comes up that isn't included— but you think should be—take a moment to think it through. You might find it does belong, and you need to revise your plan. Or you might realize it is only busywork, or perhaps it is your busy mind trying to complicate your life. The purpose of this step is simply to allow the guidance you have received to manifest into reality.

If you choose to, you can turn your milestone plan into a to-do list by putting the things from your plan into your calendar.

Here is my new milestone plan:

> Milestone #1 – Have my book published within one year for $5,000 max
>
> Milestone #2 – Develop a beautiful and sustaining garden each season for less than $250
>
> Milestone #3 – Speak, coach, and teach courses online for income of $10,000 per month minimum
>
> Milestone #4 – Take care of my body, mind, and soul through prayer, good food, and rest

I have included an example of my normal daily business plan. It is simple, and each morning I review where I am and what I feel like could be accomplished that day. I select three activities from my plan that I feel that I could realistically accomplish in that day. I almost never choose more than three, so I won't push my body back into the feeling of overwhelm. When beginning your day, give thanks for the day ahead, for your health, and for the strength and courage you have been given. Receive the strength and courage. Begin your day knowing your three things will be completed.

The key to this is to find what feels like it will fit into the flow of your day and then allow those things to flow. If they are meant to be accomplished in that day, then they will be easily accomplished. You will feel as though the universe has already chosen them, and everything will fall into place easily.

Use your milestone plan to place events and reminders on your calendar. Be gentle with yourself. Use 15-minute blocks of time. Schedule a 30-minute planning and gratitude session each morning and each evening. Schedule time for meals with your family and time to exercise.

Break down the tasks needed to complete each milestone into bite-sized chunks. At the beginning of each day, plan your day in 15-minute increments. A typical business day schedule for my milestones is shown below. Each task is assigned to a milestone and shown in parentheses. I've also chosen to identify and incorporate activities that will help to tune each of my seven chakras. For example, working in the garden is an excellent task to balance my root chakra. Focusing on gratitude balances my heart chakra. Calling clients stimulates my throat chakra. Business planning balances my sacral chakra. Prayer helps connect with my crown chakra. Writing and teaching helps my throat chakra and also my third eye chakra.

Time	15 minutes	15 minutes	15 minutes	15 minutes
6:00 – 7:00 a.m.	Gratitude (4)	Prayer (4)	Planning (3)	Planning (3)
7:00 – 8:00 a.m.	Breakfast (4)	Breakfast (4)	Emails (3)	Emails (3)
8:00 – 9:00 a.m.	Emails (3)	Emails (3)	Client Call (3)	Client Call (3)
9:00 – 10:00 a.m.	Client Call (3)	Client Call (3)	Garden (2)	Garden (2)
10:00 – 11:00 a.m.	Garden (2)	Garden (2)	Client Call (3)	Client Call (3)
11:00 a.m. – 12:00 p.m.	Client Call (3)	Client Call (3)	Lunch (4)	Lunch (4)
12:00 – 1:00 p.m.	Biz Planning (3)	Biz Planning (3)	Biz Planning (3)	Biz Planning (3)
1:00 – 2:00 p.m.	Gym/ Yoga (4)	Gym/Yoga (4)	Gym/ Yoga (4)	Gym/ Yoga (4)
2:00 – 3:00 p.m.	Shower (4)	Shower (4)	Client Call (3)	Client Call (3)
3:00 – 4:00 p.m.	Write (1)	Write (1)	Write (1)	Write (1)

4:00 – 5:00 p.m.	Write (1)	Write (1)	Write (1)	Write (1)
5:00 – 6:00 p.m.	Meal Prep (4)	Meal Prep (4)	Dinner (4)	Dinner (4)
6:00 – 7:00 p.m.	Walk (4)	Walk (4)	Clean/ Chores (4)	Clean/ Chores (4)
7:00 – 8:00 p.m.	Teach (3)	Teach (3)	Teach (3)	Teach (3)
8:00 – 9:00 p.m.	Family (4)	Family (4)	Family (4)	Family (4)
9:00 – 10:00 p.m.	Review Day (3)	Review Day (3)	Gratitude (4)	Prayer (4)
10:00 – 11:00 p.m.	Sleep (4)	Sleep (4)	Sleep (4)	Sleep (4)

Table 13 Example of a Normal Business Day

There will be days when nothing goes right, and there will be days when you just need a rest. Instead of being hard on yourself, understand that these are the days to be the most thankful. When this happens, you are being guided to reflect on all you have been given. These are the moments when you get to look back at all the blessings, all the challenges, and all the lessons. You get to reflect upon and give thanks for your journey and your life. This is the gift you have been given to enjoy.

Each evening, review what you have accomplished, and again give thanks for the strength and courage you have been given. Close your eyes, and remember the day's events with gratitude. When you go to sleep, do not think about tomorrow, just smile and give thanks for the day you have enjoyed. Even if things did not go exactly as planned, give thanks for all you learned.

The next morning, review your day again, and if something was not accomplished the previous day, think about whether it needs to be done in the new day. But remember to allow and not to push.

Then, create a schedule for a day when you will not be working on your business. Have one day each week where you do not schedule anything toward your goal. This is your day, for you. Still do the gratitude sessions in the morning and evening, but where you would normally be working with clients or on your business goals, leave these times blank. Don't fill them, and when the time comes, just do whatever you want.

🌱 KEY POINT

Scheduling your days with simple tasks that support your milestones will allow your goals to manifest and give your time a feeling of flow.

👣 ACTION STEPS

In your journal, design a normal day broken into 15-minute intervals using your milestones from the chapter on Focus. Assign no more than one task per milestone each day. Schedule tasks that balance each chakra, gratitude, meditation/prayer, meals, exercise, time with loved ones, and rest.

The Flow of Money

One of the hardest things for people to talk about, manage, and appreciate is money. But if your cash flow is healthy, then the other difficulties seem less difficult and your ability to simply allow the universe to flow for you improves dramatically.

But instead of getting deep into the details of accounting, there is a simple way to "do" money. The hardest part is getting it set up, and the second hardest part is letting it flow without interrupting it.

Once again, we have the pig.

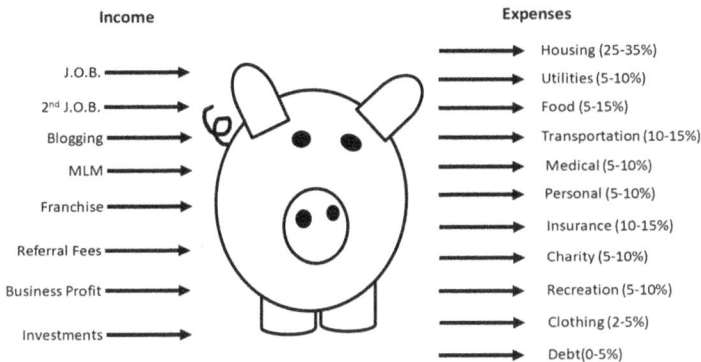

Income

J.O.B.
2nd J.O.B.
Blogging
MLM
Franchise
Referral Fees
Business Profit
Investments

Expenses

Housing (25-35%)
Utilities (5-10%)
Food (5-15%)
Transportation (10-15%)
Medical (5-10%)
Personal (5-10%)
Insurance (10-15%)
Charity (5-10%)
Recreation (5-10%)
Clothing (2-5%)
Debt(0-5%)

Figure 14 Feed the Pig

Step 1: Determine your average monthly take-home income based on the past three months.

Step 2: Calculate the range permitted for each of the expenses. Create a spreadsheet as shown below for your Feed the Pig analysis.

Step 3: Based on the past three months, determine your average for each of the expense categories listed on the right side of the pig, and determine if they are within the suggested percentages. Note that if you are on the high end of each of the expenses, your pig will never have enough to eat, and you must change the way you are spending your money so that the ranges fall in line with where they are supposed to be.

Step 4: Each month, schedule the payments for bills with fixed amounts to be automatically sent from your checking account (e.g., mortgage, utilities, insurance). For the expenses that vary from month to month (e.g., food, recreation), you will need to use a cash system in which you put the allowance of cash into an envelope, and use only that amount of cash each month. If there is some left over, that can be used next month.

Example:

If your monthly take-home income is $7600,

and your average monthly food cost is $425,

then your food expense is 5.6% (divide 425 by 7600 and multiply by 100).

Take-Home Income		**$7,600**		
	Range (%)	Range ($)	Actual ($)	Actual (%)
Housing	25% – 35%	$1,900 – $2,660		
Utilities	5% – 10%	$380 – $760		
Food	5% – 10%	$380 – $760		
Transport	10% – 15%	$760 – $1,140		

Medical	5% – 10%	$380 – $760		
Personal	5% – 10%	$380 – $760		
Insurance	10% – 15%	$760 – $1,140		
Charity	5% – 10%	$380 – $760		
Recreation	5% – 10%	$380 – $760		
Clothing	2% – 5%	$152 – $380		
Debt*	0% – 5%	$0 – $380		
Sum		**$5,852 – $10,260**		

* Once the debt is paid off, this category becomes Savings.

Table 14   How to Control Your Cash Flow

If you find that you do not have enough income to balance expenses and income, then you must find more income, or you must reduce your expenses until the numbers work.

🌱 KEY POINT

Creating a healthy money flow in your life removes an incredible amount of stress and allows for everything else to flow.

👣 ACTION STEPS

Create a flow of money for your life based on *Feed the Pig*. How did you feel before beginning the exercise? How did you feel after? Do you feel more in control of the energy flow in your life?

What It Means to Allow

Allowing means knowing you are where you are meant to be and believing there is still a place you are meant to go. Allowing means focusing on being the best you can be in the present and trusting that you are being guided toward the place you are meant to be in the future. Allowing is being pulled forward, moving forward without pushing. Allowing is a feminine energy; it is gentle, it is patient, and it is kind.

Action that is based on allowing is much different than action based on doing. A "to-do" list comes with obligations and a sense of failure if things are not checked off the list. When you take action based on doing, you take action. You take. And the time you have spent doing is taken from you. In a different way, when you allow something to happen, it is a dance between you and Source. You are given the experience, and you give the experience back to the universe. The feeling of allowing is like being in a canoe, drifting down a stream without trying to steer, and knowing that you are being divinely guided.

I accomplished many things in my life but most of them were because I felt the need to keep moving, to keep doing, to somehow stay a step ahead of the faceless monster that would run me down if I stopped juggling those crazy chainsaws. But, accomplishment without allowing is selfish; it is exhausting, and afterward, you feel empty.

When you allow things to happen, knowing they are happening because they are meant to happen, the feeling is one of unity with Source. Instead of being tired, you feel exhilarated. And instead of feeling empty, you feel as though your cup has been filled to overflowing. When you allow, it is because you know the action aligns with your inner purpose and because you know the action is the next step in your journey. Then, your actions are based on your inner power and your intuition, and you are pulled forward.

Your **Solar Plexus Chakra** energy center is associated with the *Gut-Brain*, also called the *enteric nervous system*, which is a mesh-like system of neurons behind your stomach and around your pancreas. This mini-brain assists your intrinsic brain by communicating with the central nervous system through the parasympathetic (the vagal nerve) and the sympathetic (the sensory nerves) nervous systems to maintain neural, endocrine, immune, and metabolic homeostasis. In other words, the gut-brain is responsible for keeping you feeling like everything is okay. It's no wonder that we use the term *gut feeling*.

This is the area that tightens when you are nervous about doing something. If it becomes off-balance, then you will begin to feel either deficient or excessive and you will feel this imbalance in your ability to act purposefully. Instead, you will be distracted with busywork and waste valuable energy doing things not meant to be part of your journey.

If the vibration of your solar plexus chakra is low, then you may feel some insecurity and low self-esteem. And if your solar plexus chakra is vibrating at too high a frequency, then you may be feeling as though you cannot relax, that you must always be doing something. This is what was happening to me. My solar plexus energy was excessive. I was a complete workaholic, intellectual to others but feeling totally inferior on the inside. But, like a hamster on a wheel, I was expending a lot of energy and not producing a lot of output. When you learn to allow according to your personal power, you will expend little energy and create a huge impact.

Deficient	Balanced	Excessive
Lacks personal energy	Joyful	Workaholic
Lacks self-esteem	Confident	Anti-authority
Self-conscious	Possesses personal power	Feels superior
Confused	Relaxed	Feels inferior
Insecure	Multi-skilled	Too intellectual

Table 15 Your Ability to Allow and Flow

The physical body is required to do things in the physical realm. It is like the car you drive to go from here to there. It needs to be taken care of, fed gasoline, and have the oil changed. In the same way, you need to take care of your body so you will have the power to do what you need to do to fulfill your purpose while you are here in the physical plane.

Allow Flow	Pancreas (solar plexus chakra)
Allow source to take you on the journey according to your purpose.	
"Allow your path to flow"	

Figure 15   Allow Your Path to Flow

The main thing to do to keep your gut-brain healthy is to keep the good bacteria happy. The pancreas produces enzymes to help break down food and aid in digestion. It also releases insulin to help maintain blood sugar levels. The body depends on the absorption of the food that you eat. If you are not absorbing the nutrients from the food that you eat, then it is as if you have not eaten. And, if your blood sugar does not remain stable, your physical energy will not remain stable, and you will feel lightheaded and have difficulty concentrating.

You must heal your inner self, perhaps even your inner child. The things you are holding onto emotionally affect your ability to feel secure and creative. If you do not feel at peace in your life, then your hormones will cause your digestive system to remain at an unhealthy pH, which will affect your gut-brain and Vagal nerve. Healthy intestines have organisms that not only digest food and help you to absorb food, they also maintain a healthy pH and reduce inflammation so that you won't develop leaky gut syndrome (in which the material inside your intestines leaks into your abdominal cavity).

Foods that help keep your gut at a healthy pH and promote the health of your pancreas include:

- Turmeric stimulates the production of insulin.

- Dandelion tea is excellent for flushing toxins out of the intestines and restoring damaged pancreatic tissue.

- Licorice root has high anti-inflammatory properties.

- Garlic, onions, shallots, fenugreek, and leeks promote pancreatic tissue health because they contain sulfur, arginine, oligosaccharides, flavonoids, and selenium.

- Prebiotics (raw garlic, raw asparagus, bananas, raw chicory root).

- Probiotics (found in lacto-fermented kimchi, sauerkraut, pickles, yogurt, kombucha)

- Cherries, lemons, limes, kiwi, and oregano contain antioxidants and POH, which are linked to preventing pancreatic cancer

- Filtered water

- Organic dark chocolate, coffee, tea, and wine (small amounts)

- Cruciferous vegetables like broccoli, cauliflower, kale, cabbage, and brussels sprouts are also good for your pancreas.

By asking Source/God for guidance in healing your solar plexus, you are opening your mind to the possibility of allowing flow.

Then repeat these words to allow harmony to flow through your life:

I am guided in my journey and assisted on my path.
As I speak, so shall it be.

You can tune your solar plexus chakra in many ways:

Color: The resonant color of the solar plexus chakra is yellow. Focus on this color. Find something with this color, and carry it with you to remind you to take confident and courageous action.

Vibration: The resonant frequency of the solar plexus chakra is solfeggio 528 Hz, which is natural E, *Mi*. Listen to a solfeggio 528 Hz pure tone vibration (search Google for "528 tone solar plexus chakra").

Sound: Listen to music from the harp, cello, guitar, or violin.

Crystals: Amber, citrine, golden topaz.

Herbs/Essential Oils: Rosemary, lemongrass, dandelion, grapefruit, bergamot. Use the oil in a diffuser or rub a drop or two on your hand and smell the fragrance to remind you of your solar plexus chakra.

Exercise: Close your eyes and visualize yourself standing in front of a large crowd of smiling faces. All the people are cheering your name, rejoicing and thanking you for following your purpose and helping them with that purpose.

Meditation/Prayer: Archangel Raphael, *The Healing Power of God*. Ask Raphael to keep you strong and healthy and to give you the personal power to help you relax and allow your life to flow according to God's plan.

🌱 KEY POINT

When we feel healthy and are joyful and relaxed, we are better able to allow ourselves to enjoy the moment and can trust that we are where we are meant to be and living our lives according to God's plan.

👣 ACTION STEPS

To improve the vibration and health of your solar plexus, focus on the truth that you are always where you are meant to be. Review your simple plan and journal about interruptions that might have seemed to get in the way, but on reflection, happened for a reason. Describe the reason things changed. Were you meant to rest more? Were you meant to spend more time with family? Look for the positive reasons that things happened and journal gratitude for the guidance in your best interest.

Using the Tool

Be a Pilgrim

After my NDE, I was at a point where I felt complete forgiveness and compassion for my mom. It wasn't that I accepted what had happened or the way she had treated us as children. But I knew that she was human and that something had caused her to act the way she had acted. I might never know what it was that had tormented her, but I knew something had caused her to feel deep negativity toward herself, and she mirrored that out onto her children.

Over the years that followed my NDE, we were able to have several conversations about spirituality, about God, and about consciousness. I had known she had been studying religions and the Great Ascended Masters and had been meditating for many years. She was far from perfect; in fact, she remained cold and selfish and still believed the stories she had created about her own life. But intellectually, she knew the truth. Her studies had given her a deep spiritual wisdom I had only received when I crossed over.

When I tried to ask her about her journey, she couldn't or wouldn't share anything with me. The only thing she said was "the Lord's Prayer has all of the answers that we seek."

The Lord's Prayer

Our Father, who art in heaven,
Hallowed be thy name.
Thy Kingdom come,
Thy will be done
On Earth as it is in heaven.
Give us this day our daily bread

And forgive us our debts
As we forgive our debtors.
And lead us not into temptation,
but deliver us from evil.
— Matthew 6:9–12 (KJV)

A pilgrim is someone who journeys to a holy place. They know that there is a heavenly entity, and their purpose is to live their life on Earth according to the will of that guiding light. They receive each day as a gift, with gratitude. They know they are forgiven for their mistakes and transgressions, and they strive to forgive others for their mistakes and transgressions. They ask that the guidance they receive leads them toward their purpose and away from evil.

🌱 KEY POINT

Our purpose is to be a pilgrim and journey through our life according to heavenly guidance. This tool can help.

👣 ACTION STEPS

Read the Lord's Prayer and journal about how any feelings that come up. Does one line resonate with you? Why?

Receive

Your pineal gland/crown chakra energy center acts as an antenna to receive guidance signals from God/Source. To receive guidance, first ask for guidance. Then listen, receive, and believe.

Your antenna is the first step in receiving guidance. Prayer is the easiest way to connect directly with Source and receive guidance. Ask for guidance through prayer. Say *please* and *thank you* when you are praying. The angels are there, waiting for us to ask. Use your entire heart and feel what you are asking for deeply.

During and after your prayer, pay close attention to what you are feeling and what your inner voice is telling you. Be open and believe what you are thinking and being told is truly what you are being told. Remember that there might not be words, but there will be a strong knowing. You might not entirely understand what it means right away, but be open for the understanding to come to you in time.

Our ability to receive guidance requires that we care for our pineal gland and have faith that God/Source and the angels are there, waiting for us to believe.

🌱 KEY POINT
Guidance is received through your pineal gland and crown chakra energy center. Prayer is the way to ask for guidance. Faith is the way to receive that guidance.

👣 ACTION STEPS
Sit in a quiet place and close your eyes. Then ask for guidance in a simple way. Here is an example: "Please give me guidance with (*my challenge*). It weighs heavy on my heart, and I need your help. Thank you." It doesn't have to be any more complicated than that.

Accept

Your pituitary gland/third eye chakra energy center acts as a high-pass filter to allow only high-frequency energy to pass into your receiver. Low-frequency energies may have been received from your environment or perhaps from other people who are not in a good place emotionally. Their low emotions create low energy that then radiates and spreads out away from them. If you are nearby when this energy is radiating, then you could receive unwanted negativity. By focusing on releasing low emotions and energies, and focusing your thoughts only on the guidance you have received, your life will move forward according to your purpose. The low-frequency energies are sent out through the root chakra where they are absorbed by Mother Earth.

This filter keeps low frequencies from becoming mixed in with the guidance you are receiving and also keeps them from conflicting with your focus and your journey. By accepting only the higher energies and the guidance surrounding that energy, your focus will feel aligned with your inner truth.

🌱 KEY POINT

By maintaining a healthy thought process through your third eye and using your wisdom to accept only the higher frequency energies, you will have faith that the guidance you have received is truth.

👣 ACTION STEPS

Close your eyes and think of a wonderful time in your life. How does this memory make you feel? Now think of a time in your recent past where someone has said or done something that was upsetting. How does this memory make you feel? Now imagine a door closing and shutting out the upsetting memory and all feelings associated with it. The only memories you experience are the original wonderful memories. Can you feel the good memory again? The door represents the third eye filter. See how you can now use the wisdom of your third eye to close out upsetting energies?

Release

Your adrenal glands / root chakra energy center acts as a drain, flushing unwanted energies down into Mother Earth. This function is integral to your health because unwanted energies are toxic to your spiritual navigation system. Low-frequency energy drags you down and interferes with your ability to receive and understand your guidance. It also causes you to feel sluggish and confused, unable to think clearly.

Releasing these low-frequency, unwanted, and interfering energies creates greater clarity. It helps you feel safe being who and where you are in your journey. In this modern age, it can feel difficult to connect with the Earth and release, but it is essential you find a way to do this daily. By releasing to the Earth, it helps you be more accepting of who you truly are and lets you just be yourself.

🌱 KEY POINT

Unwanted and interfering energies are released through your root chakra and adrenal glands down into the Earth. This process is similar to flushing something down a drain.

👣 ACTION STEPS

Visualize yourself physically connected to the Earth by the force of gravity. Anything that you want to release can easily be sent down into the Earth, absorbed by the planet, and never seen or felt again. Check the soles of your shoes. Are they manufactured material? If they are, then it is more difficult to release energy, so just take them off and stand in the grass. Reach out and touch a tree, the grass, the dirt, a rock. Touch nature and feel yourself connected to the planet.

Connect

Your thyroid gland/throat chakra energy center acts like a mixer, combining the received guidance with the resonance from your heart. Combining these two frequencies creates a copy of the received guidance at a lower frequency you can understand. This helps you understand how you can apply your guidance in the present moment and how to see and connect your strengths for the most effect toward your purpose. By knowing your strengths and connecting them to the moment, you will see the opportunities that will help you with your pilgrim's journey.

This is where the importance of what you hold in your heart is made clear, because whatever you resonate from your heart is sent into the mix. If your heart is hardened and you resonate remorse and regret, then even though Source is sending you heavenly guidance based on love, when the mixer combines your guidance with remorse and regret, the copy of the received guidance will be skewed. You will see the world in a different light, and you will choose your actions based on remorse and regret.

KEY POINT

Your throat chakra acts as a mixer, combining the guidance received from Source with the resonance from your heart chakra and creating a copy of the guidance you have received according to what you hold within your heart.

ACTION STEPS

Imagine you are baking a cake. The ingredients call for flour, sugar, eggs, and vanilla. But instead of vanilla, you add vinegar. How would that taste? Adding vinegar instead of vanilla is the same as mixing a bitter heart with the loving guidance from Source. How is your heart today? What are you mixing with the guidance you are receiving?

Resonate

An oscillator is a device that produces a certain desired and steady frequency. A tuning fork is an oscillator. In a receiver, the oscillator resonates at a frequency used by the mixer to create a copy of the received signal at a lower frequency than can be heard by the human ear. Your thymus gland / heart chakra energy center acts as an oscillator by resonating at a frequency that can be used by your thyroid gland / throat chakra to create a copy of the received guidance signal at a lower frequency, which can be interpreted and understood in the present moment.

If your heart chakra resonates with pure love, then your throat chakra, acting as your mixer, will create an exact replica of the guidance signal you are receiving. It will be an exact replica because the guidance comes from heaven. Heaven is pure love. Therefore, what is sent from heaven will be at the love frequency.

🌱 KEY POINT

The guidance from heaven is resonating at the vibration of pure love. To process and understand the exact guidance being sent to you from heaven, your heart must also resonate with love.

👣 ACTION STEPS

You will need two wine glasses, preferably crystal. Fill each with exactly half a cup of water and place them next to each other no more than two inches apart. With a wet finger, rub the top of one of the glasses so that it begins to ring, causing the water to ripple with vibrations. Watch the other glass. The water will begin to vibrate simply from being near the glass that is resonating. Notice the pattern of the water ripples is the same in both glasses.

Now, add one-third cup of water to one of the glasses and try again. You will see that the water still ripples in both glasses, but the patterns are now not the same.

When you understand another person completely, you are on the same wavelength. In the same way, in order to understand your guidance, you must be on the same wavelength.

Write your thoughts about this experiment.

Focus

Your sexual organ/sacral chakra energy center acts as a steering wheel, deciding what direction to focus on and what direction to *not* focus on. If something doesn't feel quite right in the pit of your stomach, this is your gut-brain helping you focus on the right things.

When you begin looking at your life from an outside perspective, it may seem as though you need to accomplish more to succeed. But that need is based on ego and has no focus because it will never be satisfied. The focus based on your heavenly guidance is clear and simple and helps you remember that your inner self knows the truth.

By creating a plan but keeping things SIMPLE and checking in on your gut-brain to see how it feels, your focus will be relaxed and calm, and you will naturally focus on the path according to your purpose.

🌱 KEY POINT

Your gut-brain knows exactly what you should be focusing on and what you should *not* be focusing on. By keeping things simple and trusting your gut, you will take the actions you are meant to take, according to your guidance.

👣 ACTION STEPS

Think about a time you felt in the pit of your stomach that doing something wasn't quite right, but you ignored the feeling and did it anyway. How did it turn out? If you could go back and do things over again, would you do things differently?

Allow

Your pancreas/solar plexus chakra is where you hold your personal power. It is where real courage is stored. When all the other pieces of your navigation system are well-balanced and functioning properly, then your personal power will feel ready to let go and allow. And then, the steps you take will be so natural that you couldn't have imagined not taking them.

When the solar plexus chakra is balanced, you can move boldly—and, like the crew of the starship *Enterprise*, you might go boldly where you've never gone before. You will go because you know that your actions support you in your purpose and in every sense of who you are and who you are meant to become. Every time you act, your personal power will feel stronger for the next time and the next step.

🌱 KEY POINT

When your personal power is ready, then you will boldly go where you have never gone before, allowing and with ease.

👣 ACTION STEPS

The pieces of your navigation system are listed below. Think about how easy it would be to allow if all the other pieces were aligned and balanced.

Receive – Receive guidance from Source.

Accept – Accept only high frequency and positive energies.

Release – Release negative energies that do not serve your highest good.

Resonate – Resonate love frequency in your heart.

Connect – Connect your strengths with opportunities that present themselves.

Focus – Keep things simple and focus on what feels right.

Allow – Maintain balance throughout and allow your personal power to take bold action.

Daily Routine

Each morning, check each of the components of your navigation system and determine how they feel. If something doesn't feel well-tuned, take the time to investigate. Perform the exercises for that section, speak the mantras, focus on the associated color, or try one of the other suggestions.

When you feel the need to take a day off, do so. Your navigation system knows best. Trust it with your happiness. But, keep moving forward. Even if you are moving forward slowly, you are still moving forward.

Keep Moving Forward

There will be times when your actions do not produce the results you wanted. Sometimes you will fail. Sometimes you will get hurt.

Sometimes your solar plexus will want to shrink back, and it will send fear to your gut-brain, causing it to tighten up. It will tell you that there is danger ahead and warn you to run and hide.

When this happens, go back through each of these sections and check the validity of the danger. Most of the time, you will find it is not real, and there is nothing to fear.

🌱 KEY POINT

The energy that flows through your endocrine system is much like the energy that flows through a GPS receiver, beginning with the signals we receive from Source through our pineal gland/crown chakra. By keeping your system healthy and in tune, you can use it to guide you through your life and toward your purpose.

👣 ACTION STEPS

Use the following seven-step practice to strengthen your navigation system. The goal of the steps is to walk you through locations in your body and imagine you are receiving guidance from Source. Physically touching each area of the body being used in the model and visualizing how that area is being used will help you learn to become more familiar with how to use this in your own practice.

I recommend that you do these exercises slowly and deliberately several times a day.

Step 1: Close your eyes and visualize all the signals that might be in the air right now. People are talking on wireless phones, listening to music, tuned to radio stations broadcasting through the air, and downloading YouTube videos across wireless Wi-Fi. All this information is in the form of wireless signals, broadcast in the air continuously. Also in the air are countless messages from God/Source, and one of them contains a special message meant just for you, perhaps a song meant just for you to sing.

Step 2: To begin, you must first receive through your antenna. Reach up and, using your right hand, touch the top of your head where your crown chakra is located. Visualize a bright white and lavender light surrounding the area you are touching. As this light becomes stronger, feel your crown chakra opening and receiving all those messages in the air. Hold your right hand there and count to ten to make sure that all the signals have been received.

Step 3: Now, filter out any lower frequency signals. Imagine that these are negative news stories, a neighbor yelling at his dog, or a woman beeping her car horn at an old man who hasn't seen that the light turned green. These lower frequencies are not part of the message you seek to receive, and you want to remove them. Slowly move your right hand down from the top of your head to the center of your forehead, just above your eyebrows. Imagine you are touching the third eye chakra deep inside your brain. Visualize a royal blue light glowing on this area and know the received signals are being evaluated by the wisdom of your third eye. Any negativity that may have been received is now removed, leaving only the high-frequency vibrations from God/Source.

Step 4: Move your right hand down from your forehead to the front of your neck where your throat chakra is located. At the same time, place your left hand over your heart. You can feel love glowing under your left hand, pulsing and warm, full of gratitude for all you have and all you are. Between the fingers of your left hand, a color begins to glow, a beautiful, brilliant green with wisps of pink, pulsing with the vibration of love. The color over your throat chakra, under your right hand, turns a light blue. The signal from your heart (left hand) is now sent to your throat (right hand) where it mixes with the received signal.

Step 5: Keeping your left hand over your heart, where the color is still brilliantly pulsing with the frequency of love, you now move your right hand from your neck down to just below your belly button. This is where you get to choose which message is yours, which song on the radio you are going to tune in to. Focus on only that song. Feel the music under your right hand, the chosen melody. The color under your right hand begins to glow a brilliant orange. This is your sacral chakra, your sacred music.

Step 6: Keeping your left hand over your heart, the color still a brilliant green and pink, you move your right hand up from just below your belly button where your chosen melody is building, up to your stomach where it immediately begins glowing a bright yellow. This is your solar plexus chakra, and this is where you take a deep breath and begin to sing that melody, the song that is meant just for you.

Step 7: And still, with your left hand resting over your heart and the colors of green and pink pulsing through your fingers, and your right hand over your stomach, a brilliant yellow streaming through as your soul sings your song, you feel a red glow flow forth from your hips and down to your feet, connecting you to the Earth and pulling away anything that could try to break this moment. And still, you sing.

Next Steps

This book outlines my signature course, Navigation for the Soul. If you would like to dive deeper into any one of these sections, there are individual courses available for each component. Each course includes online group coaching.

If you would like focused attention and to move forward more quickly, I also offer workshops and coaching packages.

🌱 KEY POINT

This book outlines my signature method. It is my purpose and my passion to share this with you.

👣 ACTION STEPS

Visit my website, GeriBurke.com, and let me know how I can support you, your purpose, and your passion.

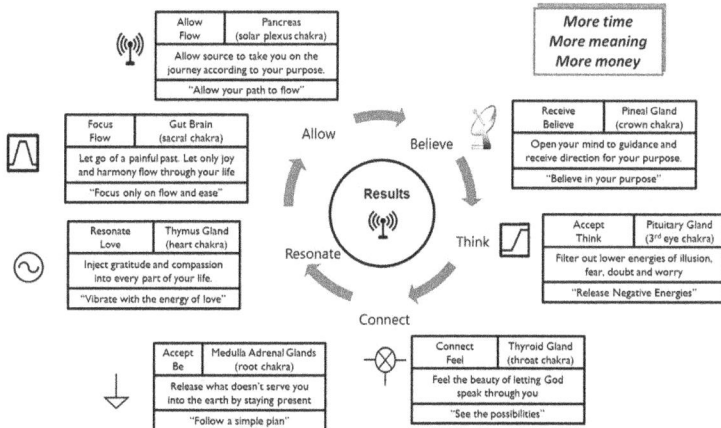

Figure 16   The Navigation for the Soul Method

For as he thinks in his heart, so is he.

— Proverbs 23:7

About the Author

photo credit:
Christina Stuart, CS Stuart Photography

Nobody knew, but Geri struggled with deep anxiety caused by childhood trauma. With two master's degrees in engineering, she climbed the corporate ladder, led program teams, and developed navigation systems. On the outside, she looked like she had it all together but inside, she was terrified that her life would fall apart.

When she heard the angel whispers, she denied them and instead clung to the life she had built out of fear.

A near-death experience changed her life completely.

Now Geri Burke is a speaker, an author, and a coach on a mission because, as she says, "God has a plan and all of us are needed." She enjoys gardening and canning what she grows on the ten-acre farm she shares with her husband in Central Florida. She loves to work with women who are where she used to be, up the ladder without a chute!

This book is her method to navigate your life and live the life you were meant to live.

GeriBurke.com

9 781736 117200